ONE.LIFE

Also by Scot McKnight

The Blue Parakeet
The Jesus Creed: Loving God, Loving Others

ONE.LIFE

JESUS CALLS,
WE FOLLOW

SCOT McKNIGHT

ZONDERVAN.com/
AUTHORTRACKER
follow your favorite authors

ZONDERVAN

One.Life
Copyright © 2010 by Scot McKnight

This title is also available as a Zondervan ebook.
Visit www.zondervan.com/ebooks.

This title is also available in a Zondervan audio edition.
Visit www.zondervan.fm.

Requests for information should be addressed to:
Zondervan, *Grand Rapids, Michigan* 49530

Library of Congress Cataloging-in-Publication Data

McKnight, Scot.
        One.life : Jesus calls, we follow / Scot McKnight.
            p. cm.
        Includes bibliographical references.
        ISBN 978-0-310-27766-8 (softcover)
        1. Christian life. I. Title. II. Title: One.life.
    BV4501.3.M3718 2010
    248.4—dc22   2010028127

Cover design: Curt Diepenhorst
Cover photography: © Simon Thorpe/Corbis
Interior design: Matthew Van Zomeran

Printed in the United States of America

11 12 13 14 15 /DCI/ 21 20 19 18 17 16 15 14 13 12 11 10 9 8 7 6 5 4

We search for God in order to find him with greater joy,
And we find him in order to keep on searching with greater love.

Augustine
De Trinitate 15.2

CONTENTS

FOREWORD

At twelve years old, I was a picture-perfect "Christian." Having grown up in a Christian home, I had read the Bible and memorized handfuls of scripture. I prayed as much as I could bear (as an alternative to counting sheep). I'd pretty much learned all the rules and had mastered the social game of behaving when people were looking. Seamlessly checking off my church's list of "do's and don'ts" became an obsession, but I continued to fall short again and again.

Questions swirled in my mind. I wondered if this was what Jesus intended and if this rules-based, internalized struggle was the sum total of faith. For the first time, I was confronted with what has become the keystone question of my life:

What does it *really* mean to follow Jesus?

Like many Western Christians, I felt a tension between the "religion" promoted by my church *and* the radical faith Jesus modeled. Much of what I heard from the preacher and those in authority over me seemed good and right, but a creeping curiosity camped out in my mind. *What would happen if I lived the life Jesus described? Would my faith look different? How could I move from a "follow the rules" religion to a "follow me" faith?*

Years later, a friend and colleague of mine asked that same question in his seminal book, *The Jesus Creed.* As I read it, a flood of emotions rushed over me. *Finally, someone has defined the Jesus way in terms the average person can understand!* He left me wanting to know more about the first-century Jewish Messiah and foundation of our faith. Through his writing, Scot provoked me to begin unfolding the answer to my childhood question.

But the influence of Scot's work has stretched well beyond me. He has inspired debate and conversation about what a Jesus-shaped life looks like among scholars, ministers, and laypersons. His love for Jesus pushes him beyond surface inquiry and his passion for Christ invites spiritual seekers into a new way of living.

Following the tradition of Scot's earlier work, *One.Life* paints a beautiful, inviting picture of what Jesus meant when he said, "Come and follow me." Leaving no stone unturned, this book presents surprising truths that will upset your preconceived notions about the Christian experience and challenge you to embrace Christ as if for the first time.

Perhaps you feel like I did as a child. You've encountered some permutation of spirituality but it has left you wanting. The gospel is your heartbeat but your current religious experience hasn't given you an outlet to fully bleed it. You're trying to make sense of your inclination towards justice and your compulsion to restore the brokenness of the world. You want to know what it *really* means to follow Jesus.

In the pages that follow, I can't guarantee that every question on your mind will be answered. But I *can* promise you that the life of Jesus will be as accessible and as powerful as it has ever been. It's been twenty-three years since I first considered what it means to follow Christ, but the question has never left me. Along the way, I've encountered competent and passionate tour guides like Scot who have helped guide me on my journey. I'm still walking the path of inquiry, but thankfully I can see more clearly.

And the clearer I see, the more encouraged I am. Not only have I come to rediscover Christ, but I've grown acquainted to a new generation of seekers, thinkers, and creatives who are on the same journey. They want life to matter but are hard-pressed to figure out the "how." They are hungry for the sweetness, restless for the fragrance, and trembling for the embrace of Jesus Christ.

I have a feeling you may be part of that generation. If so, *One.Life* has been written for you.

Gabe Lyons
Author, *The Next Christians*
qideas.org

FIRST WORDS

There are two ways to answer one very important question, and it is the question that will shape this book. Before the question can be asked, or an answer given, two stories—two of my life lessons—need to be told. These stories will tell you that I used to answer the question one way and now I answer it a different way. The answer completely changed my life.

SAVED

At six I got saved. My family had just attended an evening service at our church and—before my father came home—I asked my mother if I could accept Christ into my heart so I could be forgiven of my sins. I had heard the message of the gospel, that God loved me and had sent his Son for me and that forgiveness awaited my decision. So I asked my mother if I could get saved, and she hesitated only slightly, asking me if I could wait until my father got home from church. I told her I was afraid I might die before he got home. So we went through a short prayer, and right then and there I accepted Christ. I had learned through bold images that I was a sinner, but Jesus had come to earth to die for my sins. I had also learned that all I had to do was accept Christ's death for me, trusting Christ completely, and I would go to heaven. Through graphic images of damnation and potent warnings about eternity, I was told if I didn't accept Christ I would go to hell. My church, as you can see, believed in the real monsters—in Satan and demons and a fire stoked by God's wrath.

Our monsters were real, not like those in Maurice Sendak's book

Where the Wild Things Are. Our monsters had a mission to keep us from believing, and their goal was to get kids like me into hell. But I escaped the clutches of the monsters on the night I accepted Christ.

This is the first story and was the first lesson I learned as a young kid: A Christian is someone who has personally accepted Jesus Christ, who has found forgiveness through his death, and who is now on their way to heaven when they die.

My second lesson came years later.

INSTRUCTED

I was seventeen years old when my life was dramatically changed by a second, more profound encounter with Jesus Christ. Immediately after this encounter, my youth pastor took me under his wing to teach me even more what it meant to be a Christian. His teaching involved four things:

First, being a Christian meant reading my Bible every day—preferably in the morning just after getting up and at night just before going to bed. So I did that. Every morning and every night.

Second, alongside Bible reading, the Christian life was about praying, and the longer I prayed the more it showed how devoted I was. So I got down on my knees next to my bed and talked with God, sometimes (but not very often) for a long time.

Third, in addition to Bible reading and praying, the Christian life involved witnessing—meaning evangelizing and telling my friends that they needed to be saved from their sins. The more people I could "save," the more it showed I was in touch with the real God. In fact, the most honored kind of life was to become a missionary to the "heathen." I thought about being a missionary and had some success telling my friends about Jesus.

Fourth, the Christian life was about going to church every time the doors opened, and for us that meant Sunday morning for Sunday school, Sunday morning for the church service, Sunday evening for the evening worship service, and then often after the Sunday evening service, we had youth group. It also meant Wednesday evening prayer meeting, and at that time it also meant Thursday evening for a class in evangelism. I was at the church all the time.

I was a Christian.

There was another side to the Christian life involving things we weren't to do. The biggest ones—especially tailored for hot-blooded young adults—were: not dancing, not drinking alcohol, not smoking pot, not having sex, and not going to movies. This also meant that we were not to have close friendships with the "unsaved," because they did those things. The unsaved were as neatly separated from us as the red and white lines on the American flag: Whoever didn't go to our church was unsaved. (Unless you went to a church that was similar to ours.) My youth pastor called this whole approach "separation."

We were into separation. Big.Time.Every.Day.All.Day.Long. I was separate. My first talk to the youth group came from one line in the King James New Testament: "Be ye separate." Those who claimed to be Christians but who went to movies or drank beer with their buddies had compromised and were perhaps on the slippery slope into hades with the Roman Catholics (who worshiped Mary), and the Presbyterians (who were liberals), and the Methodists (who were worldly)—all of these, of course, were the stereotypes I absorbed in the sixties and seventies.

I could have told this whole story in a humorous way, but there's too much seriousness in this story for me, both good serious and bad serious, to turn toward sarcasm. I don't make light of the importance of trusting Christ's atoning death, and I'm thrilled for parents who nurture their children into the faith. I value these things deeply. Besides, the two stories above are from the only story I've got, and I like it. Listening to my students today makes me think times haven't changed all that much, so I want to draw your attention to what these first two lessons in life taught me:

A Christian is someone who has accepted Jesus; and the Christian life is the development of personal (private) practices of piety, separation from sin and the world, and a life dedicated to rescuing sinners from hell.

That's what it was about. If I had to choose one expression for what we were into, it would be this: *the believer's personal practices of piety.* I learned to define who I was by a single-moment act, and by what I *did* and what I *didn't do*. I knew I was a Christian, because I had accepted Christ and I was doing the right things—and not doing the wrong things.

This single-moment decision plus personal practices of piety is one answer to the question, and I'll get to the question in a minute. Before we get there, I want to observe that Jesus didn't focus on the single-moment act as much as we did, and neither did he frame "the Christian life" with anything quite like these practices. I have to put "Christian life" in quotes because he framed such a thing more in terms of discipleship. Jesus didn't teach people to read the Bible (our Old Testament) daily, because most people couldn't read. About 10 percent of the Jewish population could read (and very few could afford to own a Bible), so daily Bible reading wasn't even an option. Of course, I'm not saying Bible reading is wrong; I do it daily, even today. Also, Jesus was all for praying, and he evangelized better than any of us, and he was all for being holy. However, he clearly was not into separation since he got into trouble for the company he kept. He did the wrong things with the right people and the right things with the wrong people—and he did things like this all the time. That's why people said he was a "friend of tax collectors and sinners." (And that was no compliment in his day.)

So then, an inadequate answer to the question I want to ask in this book is whether or not the Christian life is focused on *believer's personal practices of piety*. This answer to our not-yet-asked question is not wrong and in some ways it's right, but—to tweak the words of one of my favorite Southern writers, Flannery O'Connor—it's right, but it ain't right enough.

Every time the single-moment act of accepting Christ becomes the goal instead of the portal, we get superficial Christians. And every time personal practices of piety wiggle away from the big picture Jesus sketches before his followers, it becomes legalism. And I became a legalist.

I judged people by whether or not they had my single-moment experience and by how many Bible verses they memorized, by how much time they spent in prayer and by how often they went to church, by how many souls they had saved ... I could go on but need not. Every time we get too focused on the single-moment act or our personal practices of piety, we wander into legalism and then we lose Jesus. I lost him in the middle of doing very good (mostly Christian) things.

I realize I haven't even told you what I think the question is, but I'm about to. There are different answers to this question, and it all depends on where you begin. *One.Life* seeks to answer the question by examining what Jesus says, so now I'll reveal the question and provide a quick answer that we will develop in *One.Life*:

> The question: *What is a Christian?*
> My answer: *A Christian is someone who follows Jesus.**
> My former answer: *A Christian is someone who has accepted Jesus, and the Christian life focuses on personal practices of piety.*

DISCIPLED

My life changed in a classroom when I learned a third lesson, which is the lesson that led me to the answer I gave in "My answer" immediately above. It was just after 7:45 a.m. My first day of seminary. The professor's name: Walter Liefeld. The course was called NT 610: Synoptic Gospels. On opening day a student named Tom attempted to filibuster the focus in the syllabus by saying there wasn't enough social activism in the course. I sat there, a bit stunned, but thinking to myself, "Wow, this course is going to be fun!" After getting Tom to sit down (he dropped the course later that day and withdrew from the school), Walt Liefeld began to talk about Jesus and the kingdom of God and the Gospels. One class lecture led to another, and all I can say is that it was really the first time I ever got to know Jesus or heard his robust summons to follow him.

I was a Christian alright. I was a devoted Christian. I was serious about theology. I was into personal practices of piety. But I wasn't into Jesus, because I was a legalist. I was asking who was in and who was not, rather than simply ... who is Jesus? And I was focusing on

---

* I should add that in the word *follow* we can include accepting Christ, trusting Christ, and receiving the benefits of forgiveness and justification by entering into that relationship with Christ. The focus in this book, though, won't be on the portal of entry but the kind of life Jesus expects of his followers.

what I should be doing, rather than asking what Jesus taught, if I was following him, and if I was his disciple.

That first day of class sealed my decision. That course, which involved poring over the Gospels themselves, changed my life. From the first day of that course until now, I've wanted to shape everything I do and everything I think and everything I write by beginning with what Jesus said and what Jesus did and who Jesus was. I have what I sometimes call a Jesus First theology, but I don't mean Jesus Alone—as if the only books in the Bible worth knowing are the Gospels. No, I believe in the Bible, and that means I want to connect the dots from Moses to the prophets to Jesus and then on to the apostles. And I care deeply how the great theologians of the church have understood the gospel *about* Jesus. But in that class I got my life's vision: The place to begin is with Jesus, because he is the center of God's revelation to us.

That was 1976. It's now 2010. For thirty-four years I've studied the Gospels and have come to these three convictions:

1. *Jesus didn't define the Christian life the way I did and the way many do today.*
2. *Jesus defined being a Christian as "following" him.*
3. *Following Jesus is bigger than the single-moment act of accepting Christ and the personal-practices-of-piety plan.*

Acceptance of Jesus and reading the Bible, having personal prayer times, and going to church are all good Christian things. Make no mistake about that. But Jesus did not frame things this way, and it's important for us to get back to how Jesus did frame things. Once again, yes, yes, yes. Yes, Jesus wants us to believe in him and receive him and make him our personal Savior (and Lord). Yes, Jesus wants us to read the Bible, and he wants us to pray. He wants us to go to church, and he wants us to evangelize. However, there's an orientation in all this that takes us off in the wrong direction.

Jesus wanted people to know the Bible—what we call the Old Testament—so they could follow *him* more closely and know *him* more deeply and live for *him* more completely. In other words, he wanted people to follow him, and the only way we can follow him is to take up his kingdom vision and let it shape everything we do. In my past, the word *kingdom* had no place. None. We never talked about Jesus' kingdom vision. Ever.

Here's a tragedy for me: Jesus had little place in my religion.

All of that changed when I sat in Walt Liefeld's class and he baptized us class after class in the world of Jesus and in the vision of Jesus and the Gospels about Jesus. I loved it then and I love to listen to the Jesus of the Gospels now. What Walt Liefeld did for me I hope I'm doing for my students.

Now in my third decade of studying and teaching the Gospels, I want to sketch in *One.Life* how Jesus understood what we call "the Christian life." If we were to ask Jesus our question — *What is a Christian?* — what would he say? Change the question to ask about the Christian life or how one becomes a Christian and his answer is the same. Jesus' answer, which he stated a number of times, was, "Follow me." Or, "Become my disciple."

But what does that look like? In one chapter after another I want to sketch Jesus' vision of what it means to be one of his followers. I'm about to suggest to you that the Bible.Reading.Praying. Going-to-Church.Evangelizing approach is not enough. I'm going to suggest that Jesus focused on other things and, as we do the same, each of these other items takes its place as a means to Jesus' bigger ideas. Instead of a personal-practices-of-piety plan, Jesus offers to us a *kingdom-holiness* plan. Jesus offers to us a *kingdom dream* that can transform us to the very core of our being.

His vision is so big we are called to give our entire lives to it.

His vision is so big it swallows up our dreams.

ONE.LIFE

It was August of 1972, and I was sitting in my first college class. It was called, if I remember right, Bible 101. The teacher's name was Joe Crawford. His lectures mesmerized me three times a week, so much it often pained me that class even ended. From the first day of Joe Crawford's class I had a dream, and that dream pulled me into the future. I wanted to do what Joe Crawford did; I wanted to teach the Bible to college students. Without that dream I don't know if I would have made it, because it took a long time to finish all my education — I was almost thirty-three by the time I finished. College. Seminary. Doctoral studies. Jobs to keep our young family afloat. It was hard to live on very little income with small children, but Kris, my wife, believed in me and we went for it together. I gave my one and only life to that dream, even if I had some major lessons to learn in living that dream. Now, I'm living my dream, doing exactly what I dreamed I'd be doing — and perhaps the only thing I should be doing.

Students sit in my office almost every week describing to me what their dreams are, though they don't always use the word *dream*. Julie once told me her dreams. A year later, on her way to school with her mom and dad driving, she realized she no longer had that dream and it almost crushed her. She wept before me in my office, and she struggled for an entire semester until she could find a dream in her soul deeper than the other one. She did find a dream and now she's flourishing. People with dreams can fly.

When you stop dreaming, you begin dying.
When you chase your dreams, you begin to live your dreams.
When you find the dream of all dreams, you flourish.
Chasing your dreams is the way you find them.

But ...

You have only One.Life to chase, find, and live your dream.
Let your One.Life be consumed by the dream.

I believe God speaks to us through our dreams. Yes, of course, some crackpots have dreams that caution us about chasing crazy dreams. But I think you'll agree our dreams give us direction and hope. Our dreams give us life itself and make our One.Life matter. We summon courage to try something different, move to unknown places, start new jobs, and take on more education because our dreams are sucking us into those dreams. Kris and I had the courage, after seminary, to head off to England to work on my doctoral degree at the University of Nottingham, because we believed this was what God wanted for us and because our dream drew us into its future.

Where do you get your dreams? I wonder if you think about God giving you the dream you have. People who have accomplished great things were driven by their dreams. Like Wangari Maathai, a woman who wants to reforest the mountains of Kenya. Or Bono, who wants to end poverty. Or Paul Farmer, who as a college student saw the needs of Haiti and became a medical doctor. But the one who made this so clear is Martin Luther King Jr., whose dream became a speech: "I Have a Dream." I remember listening to his dream when I was a kid, and I wonder who you might be listening to right now who will become the next dreamer to make a difference. Maybe the dreamer is you!

What is your dream?
When you chase your dreams, you live.
When your dreams begin fading, hope tells you to keep
    dreaming.
When you stop dreaming, you begin to die.
When you find the dream of all dreams, you flourish.

Devote your One.Life to those dreams.

When you do, everything else in life falls into place.

But ...

But let's be real.

Tom Rorem is a tall and handsome redhead with dreams — one of which is to be a singer. One semester Tom came to my office every day before our 8:00 a.m. class. Correct that. I should say Tom shuffled up the stairs to my office and plopped into a comfortable chair, and I made him a cup of coffee and we chatted until class time as his body moved from sleep to a semi-awake state. Tom's a singer and I like his music, and during that semester I spent most of my commute listening to his album, and one of his songs burned its way into my soul. It's about the (realistic) dreams of a generation that is now officially wondering if its dreams are becoming the problem. Is Tom's generation hoping for too much? Tom sings how his dreams haunt him but they won't go away and they won't quit:

> We've wasted time we wasted away dreaming that we can change
> I'm losing hope I've wasted away the chances that I had to change ...
> But I am breaking down inside to understand what's going on
> Been trying hard to satisfy the questions that keep holding on
> It won't quit till I'm gone, it won't quit till I am dead and gone
> In my grave it won't quit till I am dead and gone.

Tom's next lines haunt the studious listener:

> But I'm too scared to go all in to give up my life and keep up my chin
> I've been waiting far too long for this ship to sail
> I've been waiting long for a song that will let my dreams prevail.[1]

Tom's honest and he's right. And he's getting at the heart of it all: The best dreams you have call for every bit of you. And they won't let go. Why won't they let go?

MY QUESTIONS FOR THE DREAMERS

Why do you think we dream? Why do you think we dream *so big sometimes*? Does your dreaming ever give you what one of my former students, Amanda Munroe, calls "possibility overload"? Possibility overload is imagining so many massive changes in the world and in your life that you can't hold it all in. I love it when my students are caught up in a reverie of possibility overload. Have you ever been lost in a dream when you suddenly realized you were smiling or crying out of joy? Or a reverie that got your heart going so fast you had to jump out of your dream? Or that fired you up so much that you had to go for a run to burn off the energy? None of us will ever realize all of our dreams, but I have a suggestion I'd like you to consider about why it is you have such wonderful dreams:

You dream big dreams because that is how God speaks to you about what God wants you to accomplish in your life.

In our reveries we can learn about what God wants us to become and about what God desires for this world. There is an old argument by philosophers and theologians that, since we can conceive of someone greater than ourselves, there must be someone greater than ourselves. Namely, God. Perhaps we can think of our big dreams in an analogous way. Since we can conceive of a life and a family and friends and a neighborhood (and a college roommate) and community and a country and a world that is vastly better than the one we have right now, maybe there is such a world that God has planned.

What God has planned can be called the dream of God, and God made us to give our One.Life to that dream of God. Jesus called that dream the kingdom of God.

At the core of every dream you have,
Behind every dream you have,
Ahead of every dream others have,
And in the center of every good dream every human has ...
We will find the kingdom dream of Jesus.
We are designed to give our One.Life to that dream.

Forget "church" and forget "Sunday morning service" and forget "Christians" and forget church history's major mistakes, and for right now just connect these terms: *Jesus* and *dream* and your *One.Life*.

What do you want to do with your One.Life? Better yet, what is worth so much you'd be willing to give your One.Life to it? I'm persuaded that the religious life won't satisfy. It leads to legalism, it wipes out Jesus, and it leaves us parched and panting for the elixirs of God's life itself. I'm also convinced that the business life and the successful life and the good-looking life won't satisfy. There is a dream behind all of these dreams, and it's the kingdom dream of Jesus.

AN OBSERVATION THAT
BECAME MY RULE FOR LIFE

It was the summer of 1975. Kris and I were in Belgium at a huge Christian event called EuroFest. I was sitting at a panel discussion and someone I admired, a British pastor and minister to college students all over the world, John Stott, was one of the panelists. A long-haired young man to my right asked John Stott a question we were all facing and that we all face: *How can I discern the Lord's will for my life?*

John Stott made an observation that clarified my dream for me, and I've pondered his answer over and over in my life. I've used his answer in countless talks and conversations. Here are his words as I recall them: "Here's how to determine God's will for your life: Go wherever your gifts will be exploited the most." I can recall the moment as if it was yesterday, and I can tell you exactly what coursed through my whole body:

> *Scot, you've got one life.*
> *Do what you're called to do.*
> *Do all that you're called to do.*
> *Don't settle for anything less.*
> *And, give your whole life to what God made you to do.*
> *Teaching is part of it.*
> *(At that time, the zeal of my legalism was part of it.)*
> *You've got One.Life.*

In this book I will argue this: The only thing that "exploits your gifts" or that taxes you to the limits or that fills your soul or that challenges you to live the dream the most is following Jesus. Some days you may do pretty well; other days you may flub up.

Christianity isn't enough. Religion isn't enough. Being accepted in a church isn't enough. Climbing the corporate ladder isn't enough.

Solving intellectual problems isn't enough. Chasing the American dream isn't enough. Finding the person to love isn't enough. Sex isn't enough. Friends aren't enough. Science isn't enough. Politics isn't enough. Money isn't enough. Clothing isn't enough. Food and drink aren't enough. Fame isn't enough. Nothing's enough. The only thing that is enough is Jesus, and the only way to get to Jesus is to follow him, and that means one thing: giving your One.Life to him and to his dream.

In what follows, I want to sketch how Jesus understands the Christian life, or what Jesus means by following him into the kingdom dream. What we will discover, first, is that the "accepting Jesus" approach is the starting point but is not sufficient. Jesus wanted far more than to be accepted into one's life. He wanted to take over, and his essential call was to trust him enough to surrender one's entire being to him. Second, we will also see that the personal practices of piety, like Bible reading and praying and going to church and other spiritual disciplines, have a place but they are a *means* to the end. They are not the goal, and they can't measure adequately who is a Christian or who is a follower of Jesus. Instead, we are called to follow Jesus and this means we are called to be swept up into something we can give our One.Life to: the kingdom of God. In the chapters that follow I will sketch the major themes in what Jesus means by "kingdom of God." These themes will show that my old answer — believer's personal practices of piety — was shallow and selfish and superficial compared to the huge, glorious vision Jesus had when he spoke about God's kingdom.

This word *kingdom* is being used so often today it's getting muddled and fuzzy. It has been internalized by some into an inner experience, it has been socialized by others into a program for ending poverty and creating better laws and saving the planet, and it has been downsized by yet others into little more than a personal spirituality. So we have to go to Jesus and to the Gospels, and we have to ask how Jesus understood this word *kingdom*.

Interlude

A student came into my office the other day, sat down, and told me part of her story, even though she came in to talk about a paper she was assigned to write. She told me she came to school to prepare to work in the field of design, and she wanted to be involved in design and marketing for the music industry. But that idea was now in her past. She had gone to a depressed and ravaged area of America, seen serious needs up close and personal, and now she wanted to do something more significant. She told me she was hoping to take the next semester off and work in the inner city of Philadelphia to see if that would clarify what she should do with her One.Life.

I don't know about you, but I love to wander in my friends' Facebook "Info" pages. Many of my friends talk about what they want to do in life. Some of my Facebook friends are Explorers and want to work so they can do other things, like visit South Africa or climb a mountain. Others are Challengers who want to change the world: end poverty, find a way to provide water for those without water, or end racial injustices. Where are you? Are you an Explorer or a Challenger?

If you could do anything with your One.Life that you could do, what would it be? Why do you want to do that? What's so powerful about that kind of life for you?

CHAPTER 2

KINGDOM.LIFE

Once a student told me her dream job was to sell hot dogs on a beach in Australia. I asked her if she had ever been to Australia and she said no. So I then asked if she could make enough money selling hot dogs to pay off her school loans and she said no. After suggesting she might consult her parents before flying off to the hot dog stands in Australia, she began to talk about other dreams for her career.

One of the biggest joys of teaching grows out of watching students move from their dreams, as funny as they can be at times, into realities. But it all begins with a dream big enough to capture the heart.

Another student, Laura, about three years ago, asked me to write a recommendation for her application to the pre-med program. A couple summers later I read *Mountains Beyond Mountains*, Tracy Kidder's story of Paul Farmer, the medical doctor I mentioned earlier. As I read, I kept thinking, "Laura would love this book." So I bought two extra copies for my office to give to students. I gave one to Laura in the fall semester of 2009 and asked her if she might like to read it. I told her to take as much time as she needed, but to stop by when she was done. Over Christmas break she read it, and early in 2010 she wrote me a note. The most memorable line in the note was this: "I loved the story of Paul Farmer and *I want to do that!*" (She clarified right away, though, that she wasn't as "supernatural" as Paul Farmer.) Perhaps no words from a student encourage a college teacher more than words like Laura's: "I want to do that!"

Fifteen years of listening to students tell me their dreams, even dreams shifting from one semester to the next and frequently growing into realistic wisdom, leads me to this: Nothing excites a student's dreams as much as realizing the thing they want to give their One. Life to is part of Jesus' kingdom dream. One of our courses, called Jesus of Nazareth, frequently coalesces with our students' dreams to become a life-shaper for those who take it.

JESUS THE DREAM AWAKENER

Jesus was a Dream Awakener. He startled his contemporaries from their self-imposed deep sleep by standing up tall and in front of everyone and announcing the following three lines:

> *The time has come.*
> *The kingdom of God has come near.*
> *Repent and believe the good news!*

Unfortunately, these words about the kingdom have become dog-eared for many of us. They're about as catchy as the Backstreet Boys' "I Want It That Way" or New Kids on the Block's "You Got It (the Right Stuff)." I'm sorry to connect what Jesus means by kingdom to boy bands that no longer matter, but hear me out: Jesus' word *kingdom* has been used so many times by so many preachers and teachers and writers for so many ideas, we forget how revolutionary that word was for the Galileans of his day. Jesus' words brought waves of ordinary folks to their feet and awakened in them a reverie of hope. It's too bad for us that "kingdom" sounds so nineties.

For Jesus the word *kingdom* meant "God's dream for this world come true." But we need to get our minds and hearts and bodies around one very important element of this word *kingdom*: Kingdom wasn't just Jesus' dream, but the dream of everyone in Israel. Pick up any of Israel's Prophets in the Old Testament, like the long and winding Isaiah or the short and abrupt Haggai, and you will catch snippets of a bold and robust hope for what God would do someday. Jesus was capturing those dreams when he announced the time had now come. Jesus is the Dream Awakener when he uses this term.[2]

When we say "Jesus" the first association we are to make is *kingdom*. After years of speaking in churches and teaching classes, I'm convinced the average person doesn't know what Jesus meant when he used the word *kingdom*. It's like a story in search of the one novelist who can tell the story perfectly, and the only one who can tell that story is Jesus. Jesus' part in telling that story is like the progression of writing instruments.

First, there were pointed sticks pressed on moist clay tablets, then quills and ink and papyrus. Skip ahead to Gutenberg and movable type. Then some mechanical engineers dreamed up the idea of a smaller version of a movable type machine in everyone's home and called it a typewriter. Then some very clever folks figured out you could design an electric typewriter, and it was such an improvement—no more swinging of the carriage and no more pounding of fingers. (Those were the days, my friend, we thought they'd never end. Thank God they did.)

Way back when women were wearing shoulder pads and everyone was wearing Doc Martens shoes, one of my students told me he had a computer. I remember telling him I couldn't afford one, and he stopped me dead in my tracks with this pushback: "No, Professor, you can't afford *not* to have a computer."

He was right, and before long nearly everyone had a PC. Indeed, the stage was set—time and history were ready for the final, climactic dream machine to arrive and it did: *An Apple Macintosh!* I'm hardly an objective reporter, but I have to say there's nothing like a Mac. Everything all the other writing machines wanted to be when they were little boys and girls is what this adult machine is. (Okay, maybe you're not biased in my direction as a writer. So, take phones—and skip from those phones that hung on walls to the early Motorola boxy things and on to those Nokias until you get to ... yes ... an iPhone. Same company. Same dream come true. Just sayin'.)

When Jesus used the word *kingdom* and connected it to the words *now* and *arrived*, a whole story was coming to the concluding chapter, much like the day a computer finally spit out answers with precision. Jesus' case then is that history is now set to shift from BC to AD. Israel had waited long enough; it was time for the kingdom to arrive. But what we have to grasp is that Jesus had the chutzpah to stand up and say, "The time has come. The kingdom of God has come near." He knew God had sent him to declare the Time Shift was about to happen.

DREAM COME TRUE

Now let's get real about what Jesus was claiming. So the "time had come" idea is clear because it means the Story is coming to its most important chapter, and it's a chapter that will change the whole Story. But now we have another question, and it's the one too many Christians simply don't ask, and I fear they miss out on the heart of Jesus' kingdom message when they don't ask (or answer) this question:

When they heard the word "kingdom," what do you think the contemporaries of Jesus imagined?

Every Jew in Galilee and everywhere else, and I mean every one of them, when they heard Jesus say "the kingdom," looked for three things: king, land, citizens. This might surprise you, but that is only because so many Christians have turned kingdom into either a "personal experience with Jesus" (the evangelical meaning of kingdom) or into "cultural redemption" (the liberal, progressive meaning of kingdom). When Jesus said "kingdom," the first thing his hearers looked for was a king, and then they were thinking of the land (or a sacred place or sacred space) and themselves as participants (citizens). This needs to be fleshed out for one reason: Kingdom is not about an experience with God but about the society of God, and this society is Jewish (and biblical) to the core.

First, especially if you are a first-century Jew, kingdom means there is a *king*. To have a kingdom, you have to have a king. That means goodbye to the Roman presence and goodbye to the corrupt, mixed-heritage local kings like Herod Antipas. Another word for *king* in Jesus' Jewish world — and I'm not sure Christians think of this as quickly as they should — is *Messiah*. When Jesus claims the kingdom has arrived, there is an immediate correlation of high blood pressure for the Herodians and heart-pounding joy for the Galilean peasants who know their day has (finally) arrived. Next, every one of Jesus' contemporaries connects kingdom to the *land* where the king exercises his kingly rule. The contemporaries of Jesus know the Messiah will sit atop a throne in Jerusalem and rule the land. They know the land will flow with milk and honey and grapes (good ones, as at the wedding in Cana) and everyone will own a plot of that land and they will all have good crops and good neighbors and they will all follow the Torah. Finally, every Jewish listener thought of the *citizens* who love the King and who serve the King and who work for the King and his kingdom in the land of Israel. On top of this, as is known from the first promises to Abraham through the whole of the Bible, Israel had a mission to bless the nations, and Jesus was summoning his disciples to become that blessing.

We need to shed our unearthly and nonsocial and idealistic and romantic and uber-spiritual visions of kingdom and get back to what Jesus meant. By kingdom, Jesus means: *God's Dream Society on earth, spreading out from the land of Israel to encompass the whole world.* In our terms today, Jesus was ultimately talking about the Church as the partial and imperfect manifestation of the kingdom of God. What this means is so important: When Jesus was talking about the kingdom of God, he was thinking of concrete realities on the earth, he was thinking of the Church being the embodiment of the Jesus dream, and he was thinking of you and I living together in a community as we should.

THE DREAM: SOCIETY OR PERSONAL SPIRITUALITY?

If you grew up in a church, you might be surprised that I say Jesus uses the word *kingdom* to refer to God's Dream Society on earth. Around about the nineteenth century the more progressive side of the Church (now called "liberalism") converted Jesus' message about the kingdom into the inner experience of God's personal rule in one's life, and they urged their culture to adopt the big ideas of Jesus in order to transform culture. The oddest thing then happened. Evangelical Christians, who have always pushed hard *against* the liberals, picked up what the liberals were teaching; but they connected Jesus' message of kingdom with the experience of personal conversion, to that single-moment acceptance of Christ. This led to a widespread conviction, held both by liberals and conservatives, that *kingdom* means "God's personal rule in the heart of the individual." Kingdom became an inner experience of God; some people have reduced it to the nearly meaningless word *spirituality*.

This unfortunate agreement of the traditionalist and the progressive gets things exactly backwards. Jesus surely did call folks to personal religious faith, but that word *kingdom* meant something else for him. It was about God's society on earth. Transforming Jesus' powerful, full-orbed God's-Dream-Society vision into a personal-religion vision sucks the life out of the word *kingdom*.

The Lord's Prayer, Jesus' most important prayer for expressing his mission, says this: "May your will be done *on earth* as it is in heaven." That line is preceded by this one: "May your kingdom come." These two requests are to be read together: God's kingdom coming means God's will being done *on earth* — in a society, and this kingdom society is what the Church is called to embody. I want now to appeal to a custom and a term in Africa that might shed some light on what Jesus means by kingdom.

GOD'S DREAM: UBUNTU

It is easier to visit South Africa for a few weeks, as Kris and I have done, and think you know enough to write about it than it is to live in South Africa your whole life, which we have not done, and understand it. With that warning ringing around in my own head, let me speak of something we experienced: something ties Africans together. There is something that gives them one history, a powerful memory and identity, and something that gives them hope and a dream. That something is found in the word *Ubuntu* and it is one of the finest words in the world.[3]

This Bantu word comes from a saying: *Umuntu ngumuntu ngabantu*. That is, "A person is a person through [other] persons." We need to emphasize this profound African wisdom:

A person is a person through other persons.

We perhaps need to tack this saying on our mirror or on our computer or on our bedroom wall:

A person is a person
through
other persons.

We are not alone, and we run the risk of ruining ourselves if we try to be alone. We are designed to connect to others who are also designed to connect. *Ubuntu* teaches us that life society works only when humans live out their connectedness, and that kind of connectedness with God and others, and with our past and our future, is what Jesus means when he says "kingdom."

Archbishop Desmond Tutu, who helped lead South Africa from apartheid into a more just society, defines *Ubuntu*:

One of the sayings in our country is Ubuntu: *the essence of being human. Ubuntu speaks particularly about the fact that you can't exist as a human being in isolation. It speaks about our interconnectedness. You can't be human all by yourself, and when you have this quality— Ubuntu—you are known for your generosity.*
We think of ourselves far too frequently as just individuals, separated from one another, whereas you are connected and what you do affects the whole world. When you do well, it spreads out; it is for the whole of humanity.[4]

Through that amazingly peaceful transition in South Africa, Tutu stood next to Nelson Mandela, who defined *Ubuntu* with a more concrete illustration:

A traveler through a country would stop at a village, and he didn't have to ask for food or for water. Once he stops, the people give him food, entertain him. That is one aspect of Ubuntu, but it will have various aspects. Ubuntu does not mean people should not address themselves. The question therefore is: Are you going to do so in order to enable the community around you to be able to improve?[5]

What does *Ubuntu* have to do with Jesus? When Jesus said "kingdom" he envisioned a *society* characterized by *ubuntu*, and he envisioned God's people living before God and with others in a way that embodied the will of God in a new kind of society. Thus,

> Kingdom is an interconnected society;
> Kingdom is a society noted by caring for others;
> Kingdom is a society shaped by justice;
> Kingdom is a society empowered by love;
> Kingdom is a society dwelling in peace;
> Kingdom is a society flowing with wisdom;
> Kingdom is a society that knows its history;
> Kingdom is a society living out its memory;
> Kingdom is a society that values society;
> Kingdom is a society that cares about its future.

This is what I think we miss when we turn kingdom into personal and private spirituality: Jesus chose one of the most social terms he could find to express what God was now doing. Jesus didn't choose "personal relationship with God" but instead he chose the term *kingdom*. He did so because his dream was of a kingdom on earth, a society where God's will flowed like rivers of good wine.

This understanding of kingdom is at the center of everything I learned and everything I've been teaching. If you want to know how Jesus understands the Christian life, the place to begin is with what he means by kingdom of God. That's where Jesus himself began. So the first line I'd add to answer our question is this:

A Christian is someone who follows Jesus by devoting his or her One. Life to the kingdom vision of Jesus.

Christianity that saves my soul, Christianity that makes my inner filament glow, and Christianity that is personal spirituality is not the full kingdom Jesus announced. Christianity that is only about me and for me and concerns me—and in which I spend my time assessing how I am growing in my personal relationship with God—lacks the central society-focus of Jesus. That form of Christianity is not kingdom.

That form of Christianity doesn't deserve your One.Life.

But the *Ubuntu* kingdom vision of Jesus summons both our inner life and our entire being, capturing us and tossing us into a vision that is spiritually sustainable.

Interlude

Prayers are one of the surest locations to find a person's dreams, and this is especially true with Jesus. His most famous prayer, called either the Lord's Prayer or the Our Father, perfectly expresses the dream of Jesus. I learned the Lord's Prayer as a child in the King James Version, and I continue to say it daily in that version.

There are two parts to his dream: the God part and the human part. In the first he speaks directly to God with "thy" and in the second he speaks for others in "us." His dream was both about God and about others.

I recommend you memorize the Lord's Prayer and keep it in mind constantly as you read this book. You might even think of writing it down on a piece of paper and using that paper as your bookmark. You might be surprised how often the requests of the Lord's Prayer emerge in the themes central to his vision and dream.

> Our Father which art in heaven,
> Hallowed be thy name.
> Thy kingdom come,
> Thy will be done in earth, as it is in heaven.
> Give us this day our daily bread.
> And forgive us our debts, as we forgive our debtors.
> And lead us not into temptation, but deliver us from evil:
> For thine is the kingdom, and the power, and the glory, for ever.
> Amen.

CHAPTER 3

IMAGINED LIFE

To comprehend Jesus' vision of the kingdom of God and to live that kingdom life means we have to have a good imagination. What is your favorite novel or short story? Since I can't hear your answer, I'll tell you mine. I'm going to cheat because I can't reduce the answer to one book. I like Mark Twain's *The Adventures of Tom Sawyer*, Ernest Hemingway's *The Old Man and the Sea*, and Charles Dickens' *A Christmas Carol*. None of my novel-expert friends thinks my choice of *Tom Sawyer* over *Huckleberry Finn* is right, but there it is: I like the capers of the young Tom more than the serious Huck and Jim-the-Slave story. When it comes to short stories, hands-down-no-hesitations it has to be Flannery O'Connor's "Parker's Back." I don't know about you, but I reread my favorite books, and I've read each of these many times and I find something new each time I read them.

Why? Each of these works of fiction ushers me into a world where I can imagine my way into and out of situations. Even more, though, each of them lengthens the horizons of my life and expands my vision of what life can be. From Twain, I learn the joy of capers and frolicking and fun. From Hemingway, that we may battle and win and have nothing to show for it, but the battle was worth it. From Dickens, that miserly and miserable humans can be transformed. And from O'Connor, that religious legalism creates violence, and that a messed-up man can experience the grace of God and exhibit the character of Christ.

Fiction works because of our imaginations. Fiction, in fact, begins in the imagination of its author.

Jesus, too, used fiction, but he had a special use of fiction we call *parables*. Too many Bible readers think Jesus' parables are cute little illustrations of his teachings, and they are seriously mistaken. Those who treat his white-hot imaginative stories as little more than illustrations will deprive themselves of an opportunity to set their own imagination on fire.

Have you ever asked yourself why Jesus told parables, these uber-short stories? Jesus preaches the kingdom of God, but we want to know what that looks like. To reveal what the kingdom of God is like, Jesus tells parables. And these parables usher his listeners and readers into a world he called kingdom. Sometimes his stories are only a few lines, but they give us a concrete, unforgettable image, one that won't let us go. But there's something powerfully different about Jesus' little short-story parables: His parables draw us into the kingdom world and then they set us back down in this world hungering for more, hungering for a kingdom kind of world now.

Every time I read the parables of Jesus — and my professorial vocation of teaching Jesus of Nazareth means I read them often — I am taken back to my early days where I focused too much on personal practices of piety, and then I am challenged once again to see that Jesus' dream is so much bigger than anything I ever imagined. Jesus never told a personal-practices-of-piety parable; he never imagined a world where everyone got up and read their Bibles and gathered in prayer groups or sang in choirs. Once again, these things are fine, but Jesus' Imagined.Life is about other things. Following Jesus means giving our One.Life to these things and learning to read our Bibles and pray so we can live the Kingdom.Life. Jesus gets down to kingdom basics in his parables, and I want to sketch now a few of his major ideas that emerge from his imaginative short stories called parables. Have you ever wondered what the religion of Jesus would look like if we just had Jesus' parables? You might be surprised by the kingdom vision that is created by these stories. I will limit this sketch to eight ideas, but each of these gives a glimpse of what Jesus means by following him and what the Christian life is all about.

GOD IS AT WORK IN YOUR ORDINARY WORK

Imagine a world, Jesus tells us, where a man scatters seed on the ground, and whether he works or sleeps, that seed somehow germinates and grows and produces grain. And then he harvests it, and they can bake bread for the family and live another year. Very common story. Hardly worth thinking about. Until Jesus gets ahold of it. Jesus wants his listeners to see that the kingdom of God is at work in the ordinariness of everyday life. God is at work, God is at work, God is at work—in the most ordinary of things we do. When you make that cup of coffee at the café, when you teach those kids how to read, when you do that ordinary assignment, and when you carry about life in the only way you can because that's the way life works—God is at work.

Like my wife, Kris, a psychologist who sits in her office listening to others pour out their hearts—day after day, month after month, year after year. Ordinary work is where God is at work.

THE LITTLE IS LARGE

Imagine a world, Jesus tells us, where a man plants a tiny mustard seed that grows up into a big enough bush that birds can make nests and dwell in it. Mustard seed growth was an experience so common no one even noticed it. Except Jesus. Jesus wants us to imagine a world in which our small actions are seen as significant actions. Offering someone a cup of cold water, opening the door of welcome, a short note of encouragement, a gentle word of help, a warm embrace, the washing of a sick person's feet, the tending to a dying neighbor, a friendly tweet or adding someone as a friend on Facebook ... these are the little mustard seeds that can have large consequences. If we develop a kingdom vision, we will know our little actions swell into kingdom significance.

Like Judy and Dick, who spent months going to their neighbor's home every day—a dying old man with no family—and they cared for him and nursed him and loved on him and took care of his funeral and stayed with him until it was all over.

KINGDOM FOLKS COEXISTING IN PEACE WITH NON-KINGDOM PEOPLE

Imagine a world, Jesus tells us, where wheat and weeds grow together but where farmers are not permitted to rip up the weeds because, if they do, they may damage the wheat. Because the meaning of this parable was more difficult to see, Jesus explained it as a parable that taught kingdom people and non-kingdom people were to coexist peacefully until the end when God would be the judge. Humans, and I include myself, have an incurable itch to stand in judgment over others or to gain power over others through violence or to remove those unlike them to another place, and Jesus wanted his followers to surrender that community-destroying tendency and also to surrender any kind of violence that follows from judging others. Instead, he wants us to imagine a world where God alone is judge and where we dwell in peace with non-kingdom people.

> There's a pattern here:
> Jesus never tells us what we want to hear.
> He is full of surprises.
> He deconstructs every attempt to live the religious life.
> He calls us to a kingdom vision by telling stories of a better
>   world.

PEOPLE GIVE THEIR ONE.LIFE TO THE KINGDOM.LIFE

Imagine a world, Jesus tells us, where people perceive just how extremely valuable this kingdom vision of Jesus really is—like a hidden treasure accidentally found or a pearl of great value amazingly discovered—and then these same people sell everything they own to participate in the kingdom. He told another two-part parable, one about a warring king who didn't have enough soldiers, alongside a story about a builder who did not have enough supplies. Both were losers. Two winners in the first two-part parable and two losers in the second. Two people winning the kingdom like excited folks who just found a million dollars wrapped up in a suitcase and it's all theirs and two losers who had bigger plans than commitment to the plans. Jesus took very ordinary things and saw the work of God glowing in each of them. What he wants us to see is that we are called to sell out to his Kingdom.Life, because we'll discover the greatest treasures of life.

Like Tim, who became compassionate for and passionate about the homeless in Chicago. He gave up a scholarship to a prestigious academic school so he could devote his time to the homeless.

Like Erica, who was overwhelmed by the plight of young school-children in my school's neighborhood, gathered some support, and began an after-school program for kids.

Like Shane Claiborne, who was shocked at American materialism, so he chose to live in community with others, to trust God for support, and to tell the world that we can live on less so others can live.

Like Josh James Riebock, who encountered the pain of young adults — pain like broken homes, school shootings, self-indulgence in drugs and technology — and chose to help them and tell others about the pains of wounded young adults.

But unlike so many, who see and hear and know but who do nothing, these four vignettes represent those who have chosen to surrender their One.Life to the Kingdom.Life — a vision that Jesus imagines in some of his parables.

GIVING INSTEAD OF HOARDING

Imagine a tragic and judgment-headed world where a rich man has so much abundance, he tears down his little barns and builds big ones to store his abundant crops. So abundant, Jesus tells us, that he quits working and retires to be a fat cat. He tells another story of a rich man who refused to help the desperate beggar Lazarus. That story juts in a powerful direction when Jesus speaks of hell and sees the rich man there and sees the beggar in heaven with God's people. Why does he do this? Because he imagines a world where those who have will help those who don't have, and those who have and refuse to help will be judged by God.

I think of these parables every time I see the homeless in Chicago.

I think of these because Jesus' short stories are so graphic and so powerful, and he wanted them to be that way so we'd wake up and help those in need.

Every time I hear these stories I ask myself if I'm a hoarder or a giver.

I also wonder what it's like to be poor and hear these stories. Don't you think there were more poor people listening to Jesus than rich people? I imagine they clapped and gave Jesus a high-five and maybe even a chest bump.

DON'T TRUST THE RELIGIOUS EXPERTS

Imagine a world, Jesus tells us, where religious experts ignore those who are needy, but religious outcasts show mercy on the needy. We call this one the parable of the good Samaritan. Jesus uses a Samaritan for this parable because Samaritans were an ethnic-religious group that lived in the area north of Judea. They were seen as religious half breeds by conventional Judaism. (The story of the Samaritans is found in 2 Kings 17.) Jesus' point is so alarmingly clear: *Go and do likewise,* even if that means following the way of this good Samaritan!

Who is responding to the people in Haiti who are suffering? Who is taking up the causes of poverty in Africa? Who is working to eradicate child slavery in Indonesia? Jesus caught his readers up in questions like these and, instead of using a Pharisee or priest as the model of goodness, he grabbed a religious outcast.

In our day, Jesus would have used a Muslim or a Sikh or an atheist. His words strike home even more forcefully and he looks through us with his all-seeing compassionate eyes: *Go and do likewise.*

HEARTS MATTER MORE THAN RELIGIOSITY

Imagine a world, Jesus tells us, where those who think they are so religious and right are revealed for who they really are: self-righteous prigs (to use C. S. Lewis' great term). And imagine a world where those who are considered the scum of the earth (like tax collectors) but who are humble before God and confess their sins to him are also revealed for who they really are: forgiven sinners. They are people with hearts that are fixed on God and Jesus and the kingdom, even if they mess up at times.

So let me ask you the question: When you hear this parable, with whom do you identify? The tax collector or the righteous man? Jesus wants us to see ourselves for who we really are, and all he asks is that we give who we really are to his kingdom vision.

Like the Man in Black, Johnny Cash, who had problems with alcohol, who took drugs and spent too many nights with too many women, but kept coming back to God and seeking God's forgiveness.

JUDGMENT HAPPENS

Also imagine a world, Jesus tells us, where there are ultimate consequences for what we do. Imagine a world where the reality hits home that some folks ruin their potential by ignoring the kingdom vision of Jesus. They get all excited about the dream vision of Jesus when they are in high school but fail to do anything about it in college and beyond, because they think it is too demanding. Or maybe they fool themselves into chasing sex and drugs and drunkenness and money and fame and possessions and power, but they fail to see that the Desire Dream and Dollars Dream fade fast. And they don't even care.

Jesus wants his listeners to imagine a world where the one who wins at the end is the one who lets the kingdom seed take deep root and lets the Kingdom.Life shape all of life. To face this reality of consequences, the heaven and hell question (more about that later), Jesus imagines a world where there is a judgment—and it's like fishing with a net. Fishermen bring in their nets and separate the kosher fish from the non-kosher fish. Kosher fish for Jesus are those who listen to his kingdom vision and let it have its way with them. Non-kosher fish are those who listen to Jesus and walk away. Instead of pursuing the Justice.Love.Peace Dream of Jesus, they pursue pleasures and hooking up, and they explore their individualism so deeply they eventually come to the middle of their heart and find that, without God, there's nothing there.

IMAGINE

Parables are more than cute, homespun illustrations. Jesus' parables are revelatory kingdom dreams. They summon us into the world where God's kingdom takes root and grows and spreads. They summon us to a better world, to the kingdom of God, and they summon us to a kingdom on earth as it is in heaven. The parables of Jesus, in fact, are revolutionary scripts that enter into our heart of hearts, rattle us anew, and call us to complete surrender. One can say this yet another way: The parables of Jesus are opportunities for God's grace to enter into our lives to transform us.

This parabolic dream kingdom begins, Jesus says, with the imagination. First you listen to his stories and enter into them imaginatively, the way you enter into your favorite novel's characters. Then, because you've entered Jesus' kingdom plot, you've discerned kingdom life in a deeper manner. Then you give your One.Life to the Kingdom.Life.

The parables of Jesus are his sleight-of-hand trick. You begin thinking about very ordinary things, like fields and farmers and workers and women baking and men picking wheat and wounded people, and suddenly you find yourself transported into a brand new world and a brand new way of thinking. This vision of Jesus will take a conversion of our imagination; or, better yet, the parables convert our imaginations from self-centeredness to love.

A Christian, then, is one who follows Jesus, devotes his or her One. Life to the kingdom vision, and uses her or his imagination to see what God can do in this world. This imagination is nothing other than kingdom imagination shaped by Jesus' parables.

Interlude

A. J. Jacobs wrote a hilarious book that was at the same time serious. He called it *The Year of Living Biblically*. Jacobs is a secular Jew, but he wanted to see what it was like to live like a biblical Israelite. Then Ed Dobson, in Grand Rapids, decided to take up A. J. Jacobs' challenge and apply it to the life and teachings of Jesus. His story is called *The Year of Living Like Jesus*.

Since Jesus was accused of being a glutton and a drunkard (or wine imbiber) by the leaders of his day, Ed decided to visit some bars. Ed describes one bartender as short, Jamaican, and in his fifties, adding that he had a small mustache that was slightly gray.

Ed, follower of Jesus that he is, had let his beard grow according to the ancient biblical custom, and the bartender said, "I like your beard." And then the bartender asked, "Why you growing it?"

Ed's response: "I made a commitment on January first to spend the whole year trying to live like Jesus. So the beard is part of the gig."

After some conversation, the Jamaican bartender says, "Dude, that's unbelievable. So what are you learning?"

The dialogue that follows is priceless, and I wonder if this is what comes to your mind when you think of following Jesus. Ed answered, "I'm learning that trying to follow Jesus is a full-time job. I'm learning how difficult it is to actually follow his teachings."

Bartender: "So what's so hard about it?"

Ed: "That's a great question. How about loving your enemies?

How about caring for the poor, the crippled, the blind, and the lame? How about clothing the naked, visiting those in prison, visiting the sick, feeding the hungry, and giving water to the thirsty?"

Bartender: "Right on."[6]

Imagine the bartender asking you that question: *What are you learning?*

Maybe ask this one too: *What does it mean to follow Jesus if we take his life and teachings, all found in the first four Gospels, as our guide?*

CHAPTER 4

LOVE.LIFE

I am a theologian and a Bible expert, and it is not unusual for people in my field to act like detectives. That is, we are critics about the Church and what folks say about the Bible. We often listen to sermons and judge whether the preacher got it right. We sometimes listen to Christian radio, and we judge whether they get it right. We are into being "right" and at times theologians have been brutal while showing they were right.

Too often we leave it there. Once we show whether or not someone got it right, we move on. I'm not proud of how we sometimes behave, but it's too often true. A lesson that I have learned each year all over again is this: There's a difference between focusing on being right and focusing on being a follower of Jesus.

This is where my old answer of accepting Jesus and doing the right things and not doing the wrong things falls short. For Jesus, everything is shaped toward becoming people who love God and who love others, and nothing less than a life absorbed in love is sufficient to describe what a Christian is for him. Any accepting of Jesus and all pious practices are designed to make us people who love God and who love others. Here's how this grew into what I think is Jesus-shaped theology, a Jesus-shaped "being right," for me:

A little less than a decade ago I was teaching a course called Jesus of Nazareth alongside a senior practicum course that involved reading classics in spiritual formation. The Jesus class filtered into my formation class and the formation class filtered into my Jesus class, and it led to a question that reshaped my life. The formation classed forced me to ask this question in my Jesus class: How did Jesus understand what we call "spiritual formation"? I began to probe what the Gospels say to that question, and I came to a realization. In Jesus' world, a central part of their "spiritual formation" was the daily recitation of the *Shema*:

> Hear O Israel: The Lord our God, the Lord is one.
> Love the Lord your God with all your heart
> and with all your soul
> and with all your strength.
>
> *Deuteronomy 6:4–5*

I knew Jesus had brought this up a few times with his followers, so I began to ponder those passages in the Gospels all over again. I saw, as if for the first time, that Jesus wasn't satisfied with a *Shema* kind of spirituality—a "love God" spirituality. He amended that sacred *Shema*, and we'll get to the details below. What he added I called (at that time) the Jesus *Shema*. Then I began exploring the Gospels for how often Jesus talked about loving God and loving others. That led me to asking how often these two themes show up in the rest of the New Testament and into the earliest Christianity. That question and those probings changed my life to a daily personal piety practice of reciting what I now call the "Jesus Creed" often. And it led to seeing the Christian life through the lens of the Jesus Creed.

The discovery of the Jesus Creed—and I'm not saying I discovered it, but that it was a discovery for me—changed what being right meant for me. Being right for Jesus meant a kind of Bible reading and a kind of theology and a kind of behavior that led to loving God and loving others. If you read your Bible or prayed or went to synagogue but weren't a more loving person, something was wrong. This is what I learned and when I learned it, it sunk in deeply: The aim of accepting Christ, the aim of the believer's personal practices of piety, and the aim of everything we are called to do is twofold or it is wrong. The aim is that we are to become those who love God and those who love others. The kingdom vision of Jesus is a kingdom filled up with people who are noted by one word: *love*.

It is not surprising that one of the greatest teachers about love in the history of humankind is Jesus. Jesus saw (some of) the religious leaders of his day as the "religulous."[7]

They had the power, they had the authority, and they were perched on the institutional seats of power, but they weren't getting the job done. Whatever you think about Jesus, you must admit that he had a way with words for the religious authorities of his day. You could say he was anti-institutional and that he was anti-authoritarian, but those terms aren't positive enough to describe the kingdom vision Jesus was offering. It is far too easy to be critical. It is far harder to have a better idea. Jesus had both. Jesus was deconstructive and constructive, and that is why he took his followers on a journey into the core of what God's Dream Society was about: the Love.Life.

FROM 613 . . .

The religious experts of Jesus' day were knowledgeable interpreters of the Torah, the Jewish law, and they took it upon themselves to discern how best to live out the Torah without breaking it. One sure and safe religious method when it comes to laws is to make more laws in order to clarify big-idea laws.

I see this all the time.

When I was a kid I was taught often that sex was sin if you weren't married. Which meant dancing was prohibited. If that ruling about dancing isn't obvious to you, this is how it worked. The "law" was that premarital sex was sinful, and you can find this in the Bible if you dig around enough. It just isn't emphasized as much in the Bible as our youth leaders and Sunday school teachers emphasized it (mostly because it was assumed).

Dancing, to begin with, involved listening to or singing along with music that had words written by godforsaken, hip-slinging sinners like Elvis. (And then came the Beatles, with their long hair and peculiar peacoats, and then the Beach Boys, with their California seductive ways. Then the Ramones . . . and then it all just unraveled with even more vulgar sinners, and you end up with Ricky Martin or Lady GaGa.) On top of that, young adults, while listening to such words and dancing, would be touching a girl or guy and holding them close, and that fired up one's sexual appetite, and the next thing after getting fired up was having sex.

So, dancing and sex were the same thing. We were suspicious about this argument, because those who were telling us these things didn't even dance. So, how would they even know? It didn't matter, they were the adults and they said dancing led to sex, and before long, we had a ruling, a *halakah*: "Do not dance." It was as authoritative as the Bible.

My church wasn't any different than anyone else's. Every religious culture multiplies rules (except Jesus' kingdom community, which reduces them). Even if their intent was good—to make the Torah doable—the religious experts in Jesus' day made more laws, called *halakot* (plural of *halakah*) to make the Torah clearer. By the time of Jesus it was common knowledge that the Torah contained 613 separate commands and prohibitions. Add to those all the rulings (*halakot*) and you've got lots to learn and lots of help to make sure you know how to live the 613. All designed to help ordinary people "do Torah" well. Or at least that was the plan.

Not everyone agreed that this was how to make the Torah doable. Jesus was one of them. Jesus weighed in on how difficult it was to satisfy all the *halakot*. Hold your ears because Jesus sizzles the religulous with these words that I pull out from Matthew's twenty-third (white hot) chapter:

> "They [the "experts"] tie up heavy, cumbersome loads and put them on other people's shoulders, but they themselves are not willing to lift a finger to move them.
>
> "You travel over land and sea to win a single convert, and then you make that convert twice as much a child of hell as you are.
>
> "You give a tenth of your spices—mint, dill and cumin. But you have neglected the more important matters of the law—justice, mercy and faithfulness. You should have practiced the latter, without neglecting the former. You blind guides! You strain out a gnat but swallow a camel.
>
> "You are like whitewashed tombs, which look beautiful on the outside but on the inside are full of the bones of the dead and every-

thing unclean. In the same way, on the outside you appear to people as righteous but on the inside you are full of hypocrisy and wickedness.

Matthew 23:4, 15, 23–24, 27–28

This might not be the way to make friends, but it is a way to make your point perfectly clear. Jesus saw some of the religious leaders as hypocrites who made too many rulings and did nothing to help ordinary folks to live them out—and he wasn't convinced they were following them either.

Two things resulted from this "follow Torah by adding rules" approach. The first one is that Jesus thought this completely misunderstood how to do Torah. The second, which follows from the first one, is that an increasing number of ordinary folks were cut off from their faith. The leaders had "othered" the ordinary, they had marginalized the common person, and Jesus didn't like it because he thought they were misunderstanding what the Torah was all about. Hence the vehemence of his words. (By the way, if you substitute the specially designed "rulings" in your community of faith into the sayings of Jesus above and then declare the remix to your community, you'll probably discover how Jesus was treated by the experts of his day.)

Jesus found a new way, a better way. Instead of obeying the 613 by adding rulings that helped clarify the specifics, no matter how valuable those specifics might be, Jesus reduced the 613 ...

... TO 2

Jesus revealed that the number two was the guide to the number 613. One of these religious experts came to Jesus, because he wanted to trap Jesus in a theological debate. (Or, in our terms, because he wanted Jesus to tell the crowd which denomination he was in or whose side he was on in a political or religious debate.) In Mark's twelfth chapter, the scribe asks this in verse twenty-eight: "Of all the commandments [the 613], which is the most important?" If Jesus picks one, he could be guilty of picking and choosing the wrong one. If he doesn't pick one, he looks lame. Jesus was ready and his answer deconstructed the entire "613 plus *halakot*" approach to the Torah, and he offers to his listeners in verses twenty-nine to thirty-one what I call the Jesus Creed:

> "The most important one," answered Jesus, "is this: 'Hear, O Israel: The Lord our God, the Lord is one. Love the Lord your God with all your heart and with all your soul and with all your mind and with all your strength.' The second is this: 'Love your neighbor as yourself.' There is no commandment greater than these."
>
> *Mark 12:29–31*

Or, as Matthew 22:40 finishes off this very same exchange:

> "All the Law and the Prophets hang on these two commandments."

What Jesus said to the religulous of his day was this: You are fixated on your *love of Torah* and judging others by whether or not they live up to your standards and your rulings, but what you must understand is that God gave us a *Torah of love*.

What God really wants is for you and me to love God and to love others, and if we do that everything else will fall in line. Jesus' words are mind-blowing and they initiate us into his grand vision of the kingdom of God. The 613 aren't understood until you understand that every commandment is either a "love God" or a "love your neighbor" command. To turn these two into 613 is to minimize the centrality of love. To see the 613 as expressions of either loving God or loving others is to set the 613 free to be what God wants them to be. The remaining 611 are merely instances of what it looks like to love God and to love others. Jesus turned the number 613 into two.

There are only two commandments: Love God. Love others. If you love God and love others, you do all God wants of you. No wonder people flocked to Jesus: he found the relational core to the will of God when he reduced the laws to the Jesus Creed.

WHAT CHANGED FOR ME

When I moved from the formation class into my Jesus class with the conclusion that the Jesus Creed was at the center of what Jesus meant by spiritual formation, something magical happened for me in reading the Gospels. I began to see this dynamic at work all over the place: Instead of letting people off the hook because they were right, Jesus pushed them to baptize their rightness in love. One example: The plot of Jesus' parable of the good Samaritan is a contrast between the religious experts (a priest and Levite), who are doing just what the Torah says, and the Samaritan, who is doing the Torah reshaped by the Jesus Creed. The Torah said that priests (and assistants, Levites) were not to defile themselves with a dead body unless the corpse was of nearest kin. So, the priest and Levite walked around the wounded man and were "right." But Jesus said they weren't right enough, and he used a thoroughly objectionable character to make his point: a Samaritan, someone considered stereotypically as a religious half-breed. The Samaritan was right by showing love to the man on the road. There it was in front of me: a contrast between loving God by being right in one's observance of Torah and loving God by being right in extending love to others.

Time after time I found this dynamic, and then I did something else. I began a practice of beginning and ending each day by saying the Jesus Creed. Then I made myself a promise that I'd say the Jesus Creed every time it came to mind, even if it came to mind fifty times per day (which sometimes it has). What happened to me is that I became much more conscious of the need to be more loving. Believe me when I say this is dangerous to your moral health, because it calls into question both our attitudes and practices.

My proposal to you if you want to be a follower of Jesus is to begin and end each day by saying the Jesus Creed, and then say it whenever it comes to mind ... and then watch what happens to your life. Now I have another proposal to make to you, and I want you to consider this as very important to everything else I will say:

The first word that should come to mind when we hear Jesus say "kingdom" is the word *love*.

In the Kingdom.Life, the King, the King's land, and the citizens of the King are those who love God and who love others (as they love themselves). When Jesus stands up tall and announces that the kingdom has drawn near, he is saying that a society shaped by love is about to take the dance floor and show us how to dance.

Without love, society becomes a chaos of individuals.
Without love, society becomes a free-for-all.
Without love, society ceases being society.
With love, society becomes community.
With love, society becomes one for all and all for one.
With love, society becomes kingdom.

The kingdom is a kingdom of love. For this reason I have been teaching for almost a decade that we should begin each day and end each day by reciting the Jesus Creed. From the moment we wake up to the moment we fall asleep; whether we are searching for or have found our soul mate; whether we are working or playing or traveling; whether we are wondering what God designed for us to accomplish in this world; whether we are serving in a homeless shelter or whether we are pouring coffee into espresso cups, our various dreams have their meaning only when they are enveloped by loving God and loving others. When we live in love, we live in the kingdom society Jesus came to create.

Now we have another line in our understanding of how Jesus understood the Christian life.

A Christian is one who follows Jesus by devoting her or his One.Life to the kingdom of God, fired by Jesus' own imagination, and to a life of loving God and loving others.

I need to spell this out: This understanding of the Christian life was completely different from the one I had absorbed and made my own.

Interlude

We've gone deep enough into the vision of Jesus to ask a question of profound significance. This question begins, though, with a cultural context: The vision of Jesus is at odds with Western culture. That's a fact. He wants our entire life, he wants us to devote our lives to the kingdom of God, he wants us to imagine what life can be, and he wants us to love everyone.

That fact leads to another fact: Jesus didn't care if his teachings were against or with culture. He gave to his disciples a vision of God's kingdom that was so radical, so counter-cultural and (at the same time) so capable of tapping into the inner yearnings of humans, that upon seeing the vision one is faced with a decision to follow Jesus or not follow Jesus. He didn't care if it sounded crazy to some; he cared only to honor God by teaching what God really wants for God's world and for God's people.

In Lee Camp's splendid study called *Mere Discipleship*, he ponders the powerful contrast between Jesus' kingdom vision and the discipleship summons to Western values and its near-constant policy of "the end justifies the means."

Then Lee says this:

"Jesus could not have meant that we take him seriously in the realm of social and political realities."

Then Lee goes on to a question, which deeply impressed me when I read this the first time:

"After all ... what would happen if everybody did that?!"[8]

Do you see what Lee is doing here? He's projecting the all-too-common response to Jesus' very clear vision: Yes, he's saying, we can see what Jesus is saying and what he believes about kingdom living, but what would happen if everyone starting living like that? The implication Lee Camp is probing is the spineless moral cowardice of so many in the Church today. That is, if we were to begin living like Jesus today, wouldn't we be crushed or taken advantage of or ... or ... or ...?

We need to stop right there and, with Lee, ask this question:

Do we take Jesus' kingdom vision seriously or not?

Maybe we need to ask ourselves this question:

What would happen if everybody did what Jesus said?

CHAPTER 5

JUSTICE.LIFE

Bono is a *Time* magazine person of the year whose life was reshaped by Live Aid in 1985, and an experience serving the poor in Ethiopia. To many people, Bono's name is now synonymous with compassion. Here is a man who has dedicated his life to eradicating poverty and lifting up the poor. "The one thing we can all agree [on]," he once told the listeners at the National Prayer Breakfast after quoting words from the lips of Jesus, which I will cite below, "is that God is with the vulnerable and the poor. God is in the slums and the cardboard boxes where the poor play house. God is in the silence of a mother who has infected her child with a virus that will end both their lives. God is in the cries heard under the rubble of a war. God is in debris of wasted opportunity and lives. And God is with us *if we are with them.*"

Bill Hybels, an evangelical pastor of a megachurch in Chicagoland, interviewed Bono. Bono told Hybels: "We believe the poor deserve an honorable place at the table. They deserve the head of the table. This is how God would see things." The rock star of U2 shook up the life of the evangelical pastor, and the pastor made this humble and open confession in front of his (and my) congregation: "I had no idea how much God was going to use [Bono] to open my eyes and my heart in new ways to the AIDS pandemic and the plight of the poor." Bono was like the prophet Nathan to one of America's religious leaders.

These words from Bono speak about Jesus' kingdom dream and about the Kingdom.Life: "I never had a problem with Christ.

Christians were always a bit of a problem for me. I used to avoid them if I could."

Why?

When private, personal spirituality overwhelms working together for the kingdom dream of Jesus, Christianity becomes personal without the Person. It becomes God without grace. Bono goes on to candidly observe: "A lot of gospel music for me is lies. There are people pretending ... everything is great. It doesn't ring true to other people."

But grace, Bono says, is completely counterintuitive. Bono today is singing a new song. It's a song of grace and justice and peace. It is rooted in the kingdom dream of Jesus that counters what you and I brush up against every day. "If that is the way of the world," Bono announces, "we have to overthrow the way of the world."[9]

Recently Kris and I were in Stellenbosch, South Africa. On our way to the airport we drove alongside Khayaletsha,[10] an informal settlement for both South Africans and immigrants. For twenty-five miles we drove next to Khayaletsha. Twenty-five miles of little more than corrugated steel shacks with flimsy electric wires strung to each shack—maybe a mile or two wide. In this settlement there are 1.2 million desperately poor people. When Jesus said "blessed are the poor," was he thinking of such places and such people? Do you think they had anything to do with why Jesus came?

I do.

Care for the poor has everything to do with being a follower of Jesus and how we understand the Christian life.

WE'RE WOBBLING

American Christians have wobbled, are wobbling, and will wobble. They can worship the God of all creation and institutionalize slavery. American Christians can preach a gospel for all and deny women a right to vote. American Christians can follow a Jesus who was poor and themselves chase the dream of opulence. American Christians can write world history textbooks for public schools and ignore major people groups and cultures like Native Americans. American Christians can worry themselves into a lather about the gay marriage debate and do nothing for the 26,500 children who die daily from preventable diseases. American Christians can affirm "justice for all" and commit injustices in their homes and neighborhoods and churches and society.

Young Christians—and I say "Christians" because the people I'm talking about grew up in a church—find this wobbling justice unacceptable, and some of them are walking away from church and Christians and the whole thing they call Christianity. One of my friends calls it "Church-ianity." Some know the needs are great and the issues are serious, so they are both ramping up their commitment to what Jesus says about justice *and* walking away from the faith.

I have to admit that, however much I embrace a broken church as the only kind of church we will see this side of the full kingdom of God, the faith they are walking away from may not deserve their presence, because Jesus is not there. Having a wobbly commitment to justice is not the way of Jesus.

Jesus was a Galilean prophet. The top two lines on every prophet's job description look like this:

Speak openly and clearly about what God is for.
Speak openly and clearly about what God is against.
The third and fourth lines look like this:
I [God] am with you.
Have courage. (But you may have to duck or die.)

Often you can learn what a person is *for* by listening to what they are *against*. I'll give you what Jesus was against, and you can infer what he was for:

Jesus spoke against authorities who ignored oppression.
He spoke against the tax collectors who ripped people off.
He spoke against his disciples when they ignored the children.

Once you determine what Jesus was against in these lines, you can determine two things: what he was *for* and *why Jesus came to earth*. There's nothing wobbly about Jesus when it comes to what he was for and why he came—he's for proper uses of power, for justice, for the value of everyone. He knew God was with him, and he had courage.

The belief I mentioned earlier, that the kingdom has been reduced to an inner experience, messes up Christians every day. Many think Jesus came to earth so you and I can have a special kind of spiritual experience and then go merrily along, as long as we pray and read our Bibles and develop intimacy with the unseen God but ignore the others-oriented life of justice and love and peace that Jesus embodied. When I hear Christians describe the Christian life as little more than soul development and personal intimacy with God, and I do hear this often, I have to wonder if Christians even read their Bibles. I mean really read them so that the utter realities of Jesus are seen for what they are. I'm upset about this, you've probably detected it. Maybe you want me to calm down or knock it off . . . and I will. But first I have to say that I'm convinced many Christians don't read their Bibles honestly enough to even ask why Jesus came. When someone does, I jump up and down and send them a letter of congratulations. I sent one recently to Tom Davis.

TOM AND HOPECHEST

Tom was twenty-six and his wife, Emily, was twenty-two. A very successful youth ministry—where the word *big* was important—led Tom and Emily to Strovsky, Russia, for a camp ministry for 150 orphans. These were kids who had hopes and dreams of a future just like American kids, because God puts dreams in each one of us when we are born. Dreaming is in our DNA. But their life wouldn't be like any American's life and their dreams were often crushed early— *decimated* might be a more accurate word. At fifteen or sixteen years old these kids would be kicked out of the orphanage, the only home they had ever known.

- 15% of them would commit suicide within two years.
- 60–70% of the orphaned girls would become prostitutes.
- 75% of the boys would end up in jail or living in the streets.

Tom himself was from a fatherless world; his family situation had been abusive. He became a wounded, broken young man, and it led to drugs and alcohol. Then he found God's grace and the Kingdom. Life, and so he gave the One.Life he had to working with the youth in Dallas, Texas. He had studied the Bible in a Bible college and in a seminary, but the word *justice* was unnoticed. Until his time in Russia when James 1:27 — the words of Jesus' brother James — first wrecked and then reshaped his life:

> Religion that God our Father accepts as pure and faultless is this: to look after orphans and widows in their distress and to keep oneself from being polluted by the world.
>
> *James 1:27*

Here he was, surrounded by orphans and swarmed by their needs for love and affection and family. For the first time, he told me one day, "I experienced God's broken heart for the poor. I was a mess." This experience barred Tom from ever going back to life as usual. In the midst of the experience of seeing Russia's orphans, Tom's own past of fatherlessness converged with Tom's future. Right then and there he pledged in his heart to make a difference. He did and he has (made a difference).

About a year after Tom and Emily procured the rights to adopt a little Russian orphan named Anya, Tom made the trip back to Russia to tell Anya the good news about not only a Father who loves her but a human father who was going to embody that love in a home. He couldn't wait to tell her, but when he opened the door to the orphanage he saw a boatload of needy kids in a dreary orphanage with only one light hanging from the ceiling. Out of a desperation born of a lingering hope, two little girls ran to him and clung to his legs with their arms. What they said was: "Papa, Papa!" And what they meant was: "Take us too!" Tom couldn't, but what he could do, he did: He devoted his One.Life to raising funds to support orphanages and heal orphans.

Tom, parable-reading dreamer that he is, has made Jesus the president of HopeChest, an activist ministry to help widows, orphans, and the poor in this world. Tom's work focuses on orphanages in Russia and in countries in Africa, namely Swaziland, Uganda, and Ethiopia. HopeChest has 130 staff in Russia and forty in Africa, along with sixteen staff in the U.S. In Tom's book *Fields of the Fatherless* he points right at us and says this: "When it comes to caring for the people on God's heart, indifference is a sin." There are 150 million orphans in the world today, which would be like making everyone east of the Mississippi River orphans. Taking his cue from those words above, from James the brother of Jesus, Tom gets it. "I believe when you strip Christianity down to its basics, this is what it means: to feed, clothe, and treat the fatherless as members of one's own family."[11]

Tom got that from James, who got it from Jesus. The kingdom dream summons you and me to help the orphans and the widows and the marginalized of this world so that justice—Jesus' kind of justice—might take root. It begins in your local community and spreads out into the global village.

Followers of Jesus are designed to follow a Jesus who despised injustice and worked for justice. Christianity, we must admit, wobbles. Tom Davis was wobbling but he found solid ground. Do you think James' words, and now the pumping passion in the heart of HopeChest and folks like Tom and Emily Davis, have anything to do with why Jesus came? Do you think justice is why Jesus came to earth? We need to ask these questions and it might surprise you what the Bible says.

Let's sum up these questions with a deeper question:

WHY DID JESUS COME?

I've asked my first-year college students this question for a long time: "Why did Jesus come to earth?" The most common answer? "Jesus came to die for my sins, so I can go to heaven." To rework words once more from my favorite Southern writer, Flannery O'Connor: "That's right, but it just ain't right enough."

Evidence that this question can be jarring comes straight from a student's mouth (which means "true" in all its shades) in an email to me:

> one of my favorite moments of the jesus of nazareth class i had
> with you (back in '97) is on day one you said: "There are 2 things
> you need to know about jesus as we begin this semester: 1) jesus
> was a democrat ..." (long pause; and many gasps from the anglo-
> suburbanite-i-gave-my-life-to-jesus-at-camp-every-summer-crowd)

"and 2) jesus did not die for your sins" (i think one of the students began to cry :)

thanks for deconstructing and then for carefully re-orienting us (and, for many, introducing us) to the jesus the scriptures tell us about.

You can tell it's a student from all that lowercase stuff. Okay, I don't think Jesus was a Democrat (or a Republican), but it is a very effective way to get the attention of sleepy college students at 8:00 a.m. Also, I'm certain I didn't say, "Jesus did not die for your sins," because I believe he did. But he *came* to do more than die for our sins. I'm sure I said, "And Jesus didn't just come to die for your sins." The fact that this student remembers this statement more than ten years later is important to me. These lines I often use in classes are designed to provoke students into thinking once again about the mission of Jesus and why he came. (Yes, I've also used the line: "Jesus was a Republican.")

Yes, Jesus came. Yes, Jesus died and forgiveness comes from his death and the God of Jesus is an incredibly generous and loving and gracious God. Yes, there's a heaven, and Jesus wants his people to be there (more of that later). But, no, most people haven't got a clue about what Jesus said about life after death, and you would be hard-pressed to find Jesus talking about taking his children to heaven with him. This answer is so simplistic and so far from how Jesus talks that I wonder if we are distorting everything about Jesus' mission by giving that answer.

So, I ask my students the why-did-Jesus-come question all the time, and then I ask them to open their Bibles and we go through a number of passages in Luke where Jesus explicitly speaks of why he came.[12] None of them says he came to die for sins so folks could get out of this body and get all spiritually suited up for heaven. That's not what Jesus was on about. So, if you've got a Bible near you or if you've got one on your iPod (check out *The Bible Experience*) or on your computer, open it up to Luke 4. By the way, I'm finding an increasing number of young adults who want to participate in the kingdom vision Jesus sketches below, and many of them tell me they never learned this in church. Here's the Bible and you answer the question: Why did Jesus come? (I'll italicize words for you to concentrate on.)

HIS FIRST PUBLIC SERMON: LUKE 4:16 – 21

He went to Nazareth, where he had been brought up, and on the Sabbath day he went into the synagogue, as was his custom. He stood up to read, and the scroll of the prophet Isaiah was handed to him. Unrolling it, he found the place where it is written:
"The Spirit of the Lord is on me,
because he has anointed me
to proclaim good news to the poor.
He has sent me to proclaim freedom for the prisoners
and recovery of sight for the blind,
to release the oppressed,
to proclaim the year of the Lord's favor."
Then he rolled up the scroll, gave it back to the attendant and sat down. The eyes of everyone in the synagogue were fastened on him. He began by saying to them, *"Today this scripture is fulfilled in your hearing."*

Luke 4:16–21

Jesus thought he was anointed by God to proclaim the gospel to the poor and to proclaim freedom for prisoners and recovered sight for the blind and to set the oppressed free. This is *why he came*. Those are his words. Jesus got his job description from a prophet, from Isaiah. What Isaiah predicted would happen is what Jesus is saying he is doing. It's his mission.

Now think of the following things and ask if Jesus' mission in life had anything to do with them:

Every five seconds a child dies of hunger.
More than one million children are trafficked per year for sex.
More than eight million children are forced into godless condi-
    tions to satisfy the perverse desire of perverse people.
More than two million children have HIV.

Do you think obliterating such things is why Jesus came? I do.
At some point in my life, I realized that some people *choose* (that's the only word I can find that describes what is happening) to ignore

these words of Jesus, and they go on with what can only be called "the Christian religion with barely any kingdom dream." They're into personal spirituality, and some of them are even pastors.

There are others, though, who think Jesus means business when he says, "Follow me." And they know that followers of Jesus (really do) follow Jesus. They also know if you don't follow Jesus, you really aren't a follower of Jesus. This seems so obvious, but just listen to many in churches today who think following Jesus is an option or the dessert or what only the fanatics manage to accomplish. Any vision of Jesus that doesn't land squarely on the word *kingdom* isn't the vision of Jesus, and the word *justice* is inside the word *kingdom*. (We need to go on or this chapter is going to get too long.)

HIS FAMOUS SERMON: LUKE 6:20—26

People love the Beatitudes of Jesus, but I fear they read them wrong. The Beatitudes are not Jesus' list of virtues but Jesus' revolutionary announcement that those who thought they were in the kingdom (the religulous) were not, and those who thought they were not in the kingdom really were. Imagine what it would have been like for a poor Galilean to hear these words, and then imagine what it would have been like to be a rich Galilean and hear these words. The first group's chests were swelling as the second group's blood pressure was rising. Here are Jesus' Beatitudes, and I italicize those who are "in" and embolden those who are "out":

> "Blessed are you who are *poor*,
> for yours is the kingdom of God.
> Blessed are you who *hunger now*,
> for you will be satisfied.
> Blessed are you who *weep now*,
> for you will laugh.
> Blessed are you *when people hate you*,
> when they *exclude you and insult you*
> and *reject your name as evil*,
> because of the Son of Man.
> Rejoice in that day and leap for joy, because great is your reward
> in heaven. For that is how their ancestors treated the prophets.

But woe to you who are **rich**,
for you have already received your comfort.
Woe to you who are **well fed now**,
for you will go hungry.
Woe to you who **laugh now**,
for you will mourn and weep.
Woe to you when everyone speaks well of you,
for that is how their ancestors treated the false prophets."

Luke 6:20–26

Every time I read these words of Jesus I wonder which side I'm on. Am I with the poor or with the rich? I think Jesus wants us to feel that tension. He came, as he announced in his first sermon, *for* the poor and *for* the hungry and *for* those who weep and *for* those who are persecuted; and he came *against* the rich and *against* the well fed and *against* those who laugh now and *against* those who are popular. This is why he blesses the poor and offers only "woes" to the rich.

These words are in your Bible and in mine. This is no list of moral virtues, but a revolutionary way of revealing who is on the Lord's side and who is not. Who is living the Kingdom.Life to the full and who is not. Who is in the kingdom and who is not. Who is living the Dream behind all dreams and who is not.

What are we to make of this? What do you make of it?
Why did Jesus come?

Surely he can't be serious, you might think. In reading these words again this morning, I feel a bit like I'm being guided by the spirits who took Ebenezer Scrooge on a moral odyssey through his life. Don't tell me, he was saying over and over, that this will come true!

Read on. Jesus was dead serious about why he came.

It doesn't matter if you know anyone in your church who has taken Jesus' kingdom dream seriously or not. The question you have to ask is: Why did Jesus come? You need to get this question answered right before you can even begin to make up your mind about Jesus. Frankly, I know many young adults who are all for this kingdom vision of Jesus, but they wonder about the Church. And they wonder about the Church because they're not too sure their church cares much about this vision of Jesus.

HIS ANSWER TO A PROPHET: LUKE 7:20—23

John, Jesus' relative and the greatest prophet in Israel's history had he not been so overshadowed by Jesus, was in prison for telling one of the Herods that his marriage was illegit. Staring at his feet in prison, he had the kind of doubts every devastated person in history has. So he sent some of his closest followers to Jesus to see if Jesus was "the one who was to come."

I'll pick up the account now and, once again, put in italics what needs to be seen first:

> When the men came to Jesus, they said, "John the Baptist sent us to you to ask, 'Are you the one who was to come, or should we expect someone else?'"
>
> At that very time Jesus cured many who had diseases, sicknesses and evil spirits, and gave sight to many who were blind. So he replied to the messengers, "Go back and report to John what you have seen and heard:
> *The blind receive sight,*
> *the lame walk,*
> *those who have leprosy are cleansed,*
> *the deaf hear,*
> *the dead are raised,*
> *and the good news is proclaimed to the poor.*
> *Blessed is anyone who does not stumble on account of me."*
>
> *Luke 7:20–23*

It's getting monotonous for Jesus to say these things over and over. Begin with Luke 4 and read Luke 6 and then read Luke 7 and you get very clear passages on why Jesus came to earth.

Why did he come?

I've asked my students this question for a decade and there is one word that rises to the surface each time:

Jesus came to bring justice by building the kingdom society on earth, beginning right now with you and with me.

WHAT ABOUT HIS DEATH?

Why, then, do we say Jesus came to die? I hope that was the question you wanted to ask. I want to turn to one more passage to show that Jesus *died to bring the kingdom society, the love-shaped kingdom that was God's Dream Society on earth for us*. His death, in fact, is the paradoxical core of God's kingdom. We'll turn to Mark 10:35–45 and I'll outline it to make the reading easier:

A dumb, selfish question ...

> Then James and John, the sons of Zebedee, came to him. "Teacher," they said, "we want you to do for us whatever we ask."
>
> "What do you want me to do for you?" he asked.
>
> They replied, "Let one of us sit at your right and the other at your left in your glory."

A cryptic answer ...

> "You don't know what you are asking," Jesus said. "Can you drink the cup I drink or be baptized with the baptism I am baptized with?"

An even dumber comment ...

> "We can," they answered.

A cryptic answer again ...

> Jesus said to them, "You will drink the cup I drink and be baptized with the baptism I am baptized with, but to sit at my right or left is not for me to grant. These places belong to those for whom they have been prepared."

A predictable response ...

> When the ten heard about this, they became indignant with James and John.

A stunning revelation ...

> Jesus called them together and said, "You know that those who are regarded as rulers of the Gentiles lord it over them, and their high officials exercise authority over them. Not so with you. Instead, whoever wants to become great among you must be your

servant, and whoever wants to be first must be slave of all. For even the Son of Man did not come to be served, **but to serve, and to give his life as a ransom for many**."

Mark 10:35 – 45

Two disciples thought they were above the rest: James and John. (Tradition tells us they were Jesus' cousins.) They ask to be co-VPs in the kingdom. Jesus pushes back gently with some words that suggest they really don't know what's in store for him or themselves (the cross). They don't get it. When the other apostles hear what James and John have asked for they blow their gaskets, because they imagined a kingdom shaped by power and coercion. Jesus calms them down and clarifies the whole situation in a most unusual way.

The disciples are acting like power-mongering Romans. His kingdom society will be shaped not by power-mongering but by self-sacrificing service for one another. In fact, he reveals, his own life will be an absolutely perfect sacrifice and memorable example: *He will give his own life as a ransom and as a martyr for them.* He will die in order to take their death upon himself, and he will, at the same time, provide a model of how to live — by giving your life for others. (More of this later.)

For now all we have to see is this: Jesus envisions a society marked so deeply by justice that, instead of using power to rule over others, his kingdom people will use their power *to serve one another in a life of sacrifice.* Jesus died, in part, to make that kind of kingdom community spring to life.

BUT YOU MUST BE SAYING . . .

Jesus is either an idealist or his followers have screwed it up completely. The former is true because Jesus was a dreamer and the Dream Awakener. The second statement is also true. It is an embarrassment to look at how so many (who call themselves) followers of Jesus don't follow Jesus. Instead of serving others, we serve ourselves. Instead of using our power to sacrifice for others, we use power to rule over others. Instead of pursuing love of God and love of others, we are so in love with ourselves or our own form of *halakah* that we don't love others, and we lose God in the chaos of life. Instead of pursuing the Kingdom.Life, we pursue the iLife. Instead of living the long defeat of the cross, we live for the constant triumph.

What I find many today are asking is: Do I want to follow the dream Jesus gave us?

I make this simple claim for this book:

Followers of Jesus follow Jesus.

Those who aren't following Jesus aren't his followers. It's that simple. Followers follow, and those who don't follow aren't followers. To follow Jesus means to follow Jesus into a society where justice rules, where love shapes everything. To follow Jesus means to take up his dream and work for it.

We can now add another clause to our question's answer.

A Christian is one who follows Jesus by devoting her or his One.Life to the kingdom of God, fired by Jesus' own imagination, to a life of loving God and loving others, and to a society shaped by justice, especially for those who have been marginalized.

Interlude

I have a question for you to ponder, and what I hope happens is that you take this question to some of your friends and chat about it and chew on it and work it over until you have a sense of resolution.

The question: Why do so many today want to wander off to South Africa or Kenya or India or Russia or Honduras or Costa Rica or Peru to help with justice issues but not spend the same effort in their own neighborhood or community or state? Why do young suburbanites, say in Chicago, want to go to Kentucky or Tennessee to help people but not want to spend that same time to go to the inner city in their own area to help with justice issues?

I asked this very question to a mature student in my office one day, and he thought he had a partial explanation: "Because my generation is searching for experiences, and the more exotic and extreme the better. Going down the street to help at a food shelter is good and it is just and some of us are doing that, but it's not an experience. We want experiences."

Now back to my question: Why do you think so many travel miles and miles and spend lots of dollars to help with justice but ignore the local need for justice? Did Jesus send his followers off to Rome or Ethiopia or did Jesus do his kind of justice work in his own neighborhood?

Another question: What is justice? Many today like to use the expression "social justice," and by that they mean they are working for the good of society. This is one of the biggest improvements I've seen in the Church in the last two decades. But, there's a lurking question for me here. What is justice?

In the simplest of terms, justice describes behaviors and conditions that conform to the standards of what is right. It is just to drive twenty-five miles per hour in a twenty-five miles per hour speed zone. But I'm persuaded that in general too many Christians define justice by using the U.S. Constitution as the standard of what is right. So, justice means doing things that conform to the Western ideals of justice — like happiness and prosperity and rights and a home. Or they use theoreticians like John Rawls and his *Theory of Justice*.

But what did Jesus mean when he spoke of justice? That is easy to answer, but it is not the same as the sort of justice in the previous paragraph. For Jesus, justice describes behaviors and conditions that conform to God's standard, to God's kingdom. In other words, behaviors and conditions that conform to love, to justice, to kingdom, to peace, to following Jesus and to doing what God has said in the Torah. To practice justice in Jesus' mind then is to participate in the kingdom of God and to invite others into that kingdom society of Jesus.

How do you think Jesus defines justice? Better yet, what is the standard of what is right (and wrong) for Jesus? Read the gospel of Matthew or the gospel of John and jot down your ideas. A follower of Jesus follows Jesus, even when it comes to defining justice.

CHAPTER 6

PEACE.LIFE

I grew up in a generation that used the word *peace* so often it lost all meaning and became lighter than a cheap paperback. We painted the word *peace* or the symbol of peace on tie-dyed T-shirts. We placarded the word on posters and paraded through major cities. John Lennon and Janice Joplin and Joan Baez sang about it. Overuse and misuse led to abuse. The word was used so often that the word fell out of fashion in Christian circles. But peace stands tall and proud in the Bible. We need to recover this sacred word and idea, because it is part of the word *kingdom* for Jesus.

The first thing we need to recover is the knowledge that peace *is a result and not a goal*. Peace is the result of years in a good relationship. Marriages shaped by love result in peace. Instead of focusing on having a good marriage, a husband and a wife who focus on loving one another will have a marriage of peace. Societies that are shaped by justice and love *become societies marked by peace*. Peace, then, should not be our goal; love is. Love is the hard gritty work; love is the way of the cross that produces peace. When we love, justice and peace bubble up *as the results of love*. People who want peace but who aren't willing to love will not find peace. People who love find peace, whether they think about it or not.

Two of our good friends got into a huge fight early this year. In April they still weren't talking to one another, and it made for some awful awkwardness when we were with them and they were in one of their snits. The man called me one day, and I asked him point-blank if he wanted peace between them and if he wanted reconciliation. "Yes, yes, yes," he answered to each question.

"Well, then," I said, "Do the loving thing each minute and ask for forgiveness when she walks in the room."

He thought about it and then said, "That's the part I'm not sure I want to do yet." Without the concrete behaviors of love, including forgiveness, there will be no peace.

The kingdom dream of Jesus leads to the Peace.Life.

At the core of the Christian life is a life devoted to peacemaking.

ELLIOT'S DREAM

One of my students, Elliot, told me that she went with her father, who is also her pastor, and younger brother to Honduras on a mission experience. "It was cool," she told me in my office one day, but I knew there was more to this story than being cool.

The year after that first trip, she said, her father made a decision to use the generous sabbatical his church gave him to take his family back to Honduras again. This time they stayed three months and those months changed Elliot's life and gave her a kingdom dream. On the island of Roatan, Elle—as she is known to her friends— encountered the kind of poverty that shocked her comfortable life in the U.S. Life, she learned, can be consumed by the struggle to survive. Forget pleasure and happiness and things—what she saw was that an impoverished life changes all of life.

When she returned from Honduras, Elle explained to me, she was "ticked" about the U.S. and especially her eighth-grade friends who wanted to do little more than go to the mall to shop. But she couldn't grip what it was that made her ticked off about the U.S.

She said these words to me as she sat in my office reflecting: "My thirteen-year-old body didn't understand that I had been changed by my time in Honduras."

Prior to the trip, she had been a consumerist; after her trip she was not. Elle admitted that she became judgmental of her friends and her country, but she got through that. Then she surprised me with what she said next, but she's thought long and hard about what she wants to do with her One.Life.

Elliot told me she believed God was preparing her to be a missionary. To do what? To become a nurse in Honduras. "I believe God wants me to be a missionary nurse. I want to help the poor in tangible ways. Yes, that's what I think God has called me to do."

So she's studying at North Park University to become a registered nurse. She's also filtering her future husband through the vocation God has given her: to serve the poor in compassion through her church.

This is Elle's dream and she wants to dedicate her One.Life to this peace dream. Anyone who loves others and serves others will bring peace into the world.

WHEN PEACE LIKE A RIVER . . .

Perhaps you are wondering why I describe the (potential) impact of Elliot's nursing with the word *peace* instead of the word *justice*. Because the word *peace* in the Bible is a big word. Here again I'm convinced many don't even bother to read what Jesus (or the Bible) has to say about peace. Many associate peace with inner tranquility or spiritual calm. I'm 100 percent for spiritual turbulence giving way to spiritual serenity. I want the inner contentment found in the image of a glassy-smooth Wisconsin-summer-morning lake all day long, and you probably do too. I believe God wants us to have serenity, and serenity surely comes from faith in God and what God is doing in this world.

The word *peace* does describe things like tranquility, calm, contentment, and serenity. Randy Harris, a college professor in Texas, says you can have "feelings of peace and calm because you know in the end when sin and sickness, disease and death, war and plague, and the devil himself have done their worst, God has the last word."[13] It is true, serenity emerges from the conviction that God can be trusted.

Yes, serenity is something to sing about. As a kid I learned to sing with gusto the hymn "It Is Well with My Soul."[14] The opening verse and chorus express one's inner experience of contentment, and recently I heard Atlanta artist Todd Fields sing this song gloriously:

When peace, like a river, attendeth my way,
When sorrows like sea billows roll;
Whatever my lot, thou hast taught me to say,

It is well, it is well with my soul.
It is well with my soul,
it is well, it is well with my soul.

I'm all for inner calm and tranquility, and for peace in the soul. I love a quiet evening with Kris on our back porch. I like the sense of inner joy in reading the Bible and praying. I want my soul to be well. And I want to be at peace with God. If I'm at a church and they choose this hymn, I'll be the first to lift my voice.

But ...
Isn't Jesus talking about more than just inner peace?
Isn't he talking about something bigger?

Which leads me to some more questions: Don't you think Jesus wanted peace between your mother and father, and between you and your mom and your dad, between you and your siblings or your friends or your employer or fellow workers?

Let's dig in a bit deeper: Don't you think Jesus wanted the poor to have food? Don't you think he wanted the impoverished to have health care? Don't you think he wanted the needy to have a safe refuge for a dwelling? Don't you think Jesus wanted countries to get along? If Jesus used the word *kingdom*, didn't he want peace between neighbors and tribes and counties and states and nations?

We have a tendency to reduce the word *peace* to meaning "It is well with my soul." And when we reduce the message of Jesus too narrowly, to an individual's *inner* peace, we cut short the kingdom banquet of Jesus and settle for dessert alone in our own little apartment. When I hear the word *peace* in the Bible, the first thing I think of is a big banquet with friends *and* enemies (now become friends).

Jesus' dream kingdom is one in which peace is central. "It is well with my soul" is one part of the story. In fact, you might even say it is a minor actor in the kingdom script. When I think of the movie *Titanic*, I don't recall the acting of Kathy Bates or Bill Paxton; I think of Leonardo and Kate — and so do you. (My apologies to those who specialize in minor characters.) And when we think of Jesus' vision of peace, inner tranquility is like a minor actor. Jesus not only wanted individuals to be tranquil, he wanted (even more) for kingdom society to be at peace. For Jesus, *peace* was a big word.

> Peace was at the core of what Jesus meant by kingdom.
> Kingdom means love, justice, and peace.
> Kingdom means love, justice, and peace in a society.
> Kingdom means love, justice, and peace in a society on earth.
> As in heaven.
> Jesus prayed for this very thing.
> We are to pray for love, justice, and peace in society every day.

The kingdom dream of Jesus is a dream for the Peace.Life, and he called you and me to give our One.Life to the Peace.Life. But what did Jesus mean by *peace*?

GOD'S PEACE IS VERY JEWISH

Once I was asked to participate in a media event where the host was about to interview me about my book *The Jesus Creed*. As we were about to begin the interview, the host made this observation. "I wasn't aware until I read your book that Jesus was even Jewish."

I managed to avoid rolling my (yougottabekiddin'me) eyes, because somehow I was not surprised. Why? Because Jesus has been captured and turned into an American. Jesus was as Jewish as *Saved by the Bell* is Bayside and *Harry Potter* is magic.

Jesus was a Jew and, when he thought of peace, he used the quintessential Jewish word *shalom*. Do you know what *shalom* meant for a first-century Jew? *Shalom* meant three things:

1. Material prosperity
2. Loving relationships with God, family, Israel, and other nations
3. Moral goodness and integrity

For a Jew of Jesus' day, you've got peace ...

When you've got what you need and need what you've got,
When you love those you're with and are with the ones you love,
When the ones you're with love you, and
When you are doing good to those who are doing good to you.

My favorite passage in the Bible about peace is found in that great prophet Isaiah, in his sixtieth chapter. He describes Jerusalem's leaders standing at the gates and being incapable of shutting doors, because foreigners are lining up to give them material gifts as global trade flourishes.

> Your gates will always stand open, they will never be shut, day
> or night, so that people may bring you the wealth of the nations.
>
> *Isaiah 60:11*

Israel will be the talk of the Mediterranean, and historians will say this was the greatest time in history to be alive! *Others* will say that Israel is "the everlasting pride and joy of all generations." Israel's prophets must have grown up wanting to be poets, because the following lines are gorgeous in imagery about the *moral integrity* of the people who are *so in love and at peace with God* that they praise him constantly:

> I will make peace [*Shalom*] your governor
> and righteousness your ruler.
> No longer will violence be heard in your land,
> nor ruin or destruction within your borders,
> but you will call your walls Salvation
> and your gates Praise.
>
> *Isaiah 60:17– 18 NIV*

Peace happens when your ruler has the name *Shalom* and your king has the name *Mr. Righteous* and when you name the walls around your city *Salvation* and when you name the gates to your city *Praise*. Isaiah saw a day when rulers and kings and walls and gates would have such names. That was the dream of *Shalom* that God gave to Isaiah, and when Jesus announced peace he was tapping into Isaiah's imagery.

Every Christmas we join with the angels to sing about "*shalom* to those on whom God's favor rests." When Jesus began his preaching, he announced God's special favor on *shalom*-makers, and when he ended his ministry the crowds sang: "Blessed is the king who comes in the name of the Lord! *Shalom* in heaven and glory in the highest!" Jesus wept over Jerusalem's response to him, because he was offering them the only thing that could bring them what they wanted: "If you, even you, had only known on this day what would bring you *shalom.*"[15]

Jesus' dream kingdom was a *shalom* kingdom. One evening, during the last week Jesus spent with his disciples, he warned them of the turbulence to come and promised them an inner tranquility: "*Shalom* I leave with you; my *shalom* I give you. I do not give to you as the world gives. Do not let your hearts be troubled and do not be afraid." Put it all together and you've got real soul peace and real social peace.

It may be cool to believe in peace and to claim we are for peace and to wear a tie-died T-shirt. But peace is hard work. Peace is the result of a life of steadfast commitment to work things out, the result of letting God's inner peace become God's outer peace.

PEACE TODAY

Peace is when you've got what you need and need what you've got, when you love those you are with and are with the ones you love, and when you are doing good to others and they are doing good to you. We need to put this together with Jesus' kingdom vision of peace. Followers of Jesus follow Jesus into a kingdom that is shaped by peace ...

But ...

We don't have what we need or need so much of what we've got: Between 12 and 20 percent of Americans live below the line of having what they need, and Christians don't care enough — the national average of giving is less than 4 percent of income. Every three and a half seconds someone in the world dies of starvation, and yet there is plenty of food for everyone. The World Bank defines absolute poverty as those living on less than one dollar per day and moderate poverty as those living on less than two dollars per day. In 2001, 1.1 *billion* people were living on less than one dollar per day and 2.7 *billion* people on less than two dollars per day. That means 3.8 billion of God's sixth-day "and it was very good" creation are living on less than two dollars per day. Take a look at your closets and your drawers and your shelves and your walls and think of what would happen if you got rid of everything you don't need.

Is this peace? No.

But ...

We don't love the ones we are with and aren't with the ones we love: About 50 percent of marriages end in divorce, and the divorce rate for those who claim to be followers of Jesus is statistically not that much better than it is in the total American population. Women are more likely to experience abuse in more hierarchical marriages, Christian or not. Racism, in spite of gains in the last century, isn't likely to go away any time soon unless something drastic happens. In 1989, Gallup did a poll that revealed 11 percent of Catholics and nonevangelical Christians objected to having black neighbors. That number rose with other groups: 16 percent of mainline Protestants, 17 percent of Baptists and evangelicals, and 20 percent of Southern Baptists.

Is this peace? No.

But ...

We are not doing good: In 2007, in New York City, a city of 8.2 million, there were 614 violent crimes and more than 1,800 property crimes. In Detroit there were 2,289 violent crimes and 6,772 property crimes. We could spread our net wide here. What about crime in Rwanda? Or is it even permissible to call genocide a crime? What about Darfur? What about Johannesburg, South Africa? What about the Israeli-Palestinian conflict? What about North Korea, a country held under lock and key? What's really going on behind closed doors in Russia?

Let's dig a bit deeper into our own backyards. How integrated is your church? I've heard many times that the magic line is 20 percent. As in, when we get to a 20-percent minority population in our churches, then we are truly integrated. Is this true of your church? Another question: What is the reputation of your community of faith in your larger community? Do the poor seek out your church? Do the wounded? Do the needy? While churches do well at times, they don't do well often enough.

Is this the way of peace? No.

Jesus and peace belong together.

Followers of Jesus follow Jesus.
To follow Jesus means to pursue peace.
Kingdom.Life is Peace.Life.

How Jewish is your view of peace? It might be well with your soul and it might be well with my soul, but what about the poor kid in Mississippi? The abused boy in Florida? The neglected child in California? The abused wife in North Dakota? The ostracized black girl in the Chicago suburb? The robbed elderly woman in Dallas? The diseased man in Alaska who can't afford medical insurance? Jesus dreamed of a kingdom society, a society where God's good will is done on earth as it is done in heaven. He dreamed of a society that in its soul was shaped by loving God and loving others, by justice for all and by giving peace a chance. Peace flows from those who act justly and who behave lovingly. I believe if peace is going to get a chance today, it must begin with or include those who claim to be the followers of Jesus. Anyone who wants to follow Jesus must follow the King of Peace. One of Jesus' greatest followers, the apostle Paul, blessed the Romans with these words: "The God of *shalom* be with you all." And, one chapter later, Paul prayed that the God of *shalom* would "crush Satan" under their feet.[16]

AMY, MATT, AND DREW

Three students in the matter of one month told me their dreams, and what they planned made me grateful to be around them. Over lunch, I asked Amy and Matt what they were going to do when they graduated. Amy said something like this: "We're going to walk Africa."

After I attached my lower jaw to my upper jaw, I asked her to repeat herself.

"We're going to walk Africa."

I said, "Africa's a big place, you know."

So they described what they planned to do: Fly to Cape Town, South Africa, and walk from Cape Town up the eastern coast of Africa to Cairo and then over the top of Africa to Morocco ("Or close," as Amy said).

"Why?" was my question.

"To raise money for water." (Their website is called Walk4Water.)[17]

So I pulled out my fatherly skills to warn them of the danger, and they looked through me like it was a waste of time and not a little paternalistic ... because these students have a vision, a vision of world peace and justice and they want to do something about it. I pray for them and I thank God for them.

In the same restaurant, another student, Drew, told me that he spent a summer homeless in Chicago to learn the plight of the homeless, and he produced a video on Vimeo.com to show what he learned.[18] I asked him what he's going to do when he graduates.

No kidding, this is what he told me: "I'm going to buy a bus, convert it so it can run on vegetable oil, and then travel around and promote my video so I can get local churches more involved in helping the homeless and the marginalized."

I had no idea what he was talking about with the vegetable-oil-conversion thing, but he did and he explained it to me. So I chased that question (and moment of learning) down with another question: "Then what are you going to do?"

"I'm going to walk Africa too."

I'm praying for Drew.

One more time: I'm grateful to be around students who know that justice and love and compassion promote the Peace.Life in the world and that they want to make their One.Life count. To show how vital these sorts of actions are for our world and for following Jesus, I want to paraphrase a saying of Jesus with a slight twist. Jesus said, "For I was hungry and you gave me something to eat, I was thirsty and you gave me something to drink ..." (Matthew 25:35).

For Amy, Matt, and Drew, we could render this, "For I was hungry and you gave me something to eat, I was thirsty and you gave me *some clean water* to drink."

The kingdom dream of Jesus means devoting our One.Life to justice, love, and peace. We are getting closer to a complete answer to our question.

A Christian is one who follows Jesus by devoting her or his One.Life to the kingdom of God, fired by Jesus' own imagination, to a life of loving God and loving others, and to a society shaped by justice, especially for those who have been marginalized, and to peace.

Interlude

The best word for Jesus' dream is that he wanted it to go *viral*. Jesus launched his kingdom dream at a wedding with friends and family. He didn't march into Jerusalem on a white horse or sail off to Rome to topple the powers that be. Instead, he set up shop at an ordinary house at an ordinary event, and he launched the kingdom dream with ordinary people.

When Jesus launched his justice vision, he summoned the sick and the blind and the wounded and the oppressed. When he called his followers to root everything they do in love, he was speaking to the ordinary relationships of ordinary life. When he launched his "community" vision, he chose to do so at ordinary tables in ordinary homes. When he showed what it was like to live in and pursue peace, Jesus didn't enter into the halls of laws in Jerusalem or reshape the law books in Rome—no, he just began living that way and asked ordinary people to join him.

Ever since Jesus, though, the Church has been tempted by another way: the way of power, the way of might, the way of violence, the way of coercion. There's another temptation as well, which is to bottle or package Jesus' kingdom dream into an institutional organization that can perpetuate his kingdom vision. But those ways don't work. The kingdom dream won't be realized by power and might and violence and coercion. That way ruins the dream. And the kingdom can't be contained in an institution or reduced to an organization.

No, Jesus wanted his kingdom dream to go viral. He wanted you and me and ordinary folks like us to launch the kingdom dream in our lives. One day at a time. In ordinary ways. With ordinary people.

Why do you think we are so tempted to capture the vision of Jesus in an institution, as if it can be contained? Why do you think we are tempted so easily to coercion and force?

CHAPTER 7

WISDOM.LIFE

The Bible tells an old story in 1 Kings that is perhaps one of the best stories you will ever read. The Bible's story is about a young king named Solomon, whose father, David, was the first, most famous, and most powerful king in Israel's history. Just before David died he announced that his son Solomon would be the next king. Very early in Solomon's career God asked Solomon a question.

> **God:** "If you could have anything you wanted, what would you want?" (Actually, *God's* question is even better than that: "I will give you whatever you want, so what do you want?")
>
> **Solomon:** "Give your servant a discerning heart to govern your people and to distinguish between right and wrong."

Solomon, who can have anything he wants, asks for wisdom.

God answers that request by putting on the table the things Solomon did not ask for.

> **God:** "Since you have asked for this and not for long life or wealth for yourself, nor have [you] asked for the death of your enemies but for *discernment in administering justice*, I will do what you have asked. *I will give you a wise and discerning heart*, so that there will never have been anyone like you, nor will there ever be.
>
>   Moreover, I will give you what you have not asked for — both *wealth* and *honor* — so that in your lifetime you will have no equal among kings. And if you walk in obedience to me and

keep my decrees and commands as David your father did, I will give you a *long life.*

1 Kings 3:5–14

Tragically, what Solomon *asked* for and how he *acted* were poles apart. Solomon brilliantly asked for wisdom, but Solomon acted like a fool as he aged. Solomon's dream became unsustainable and it unraveled. He was the Enron of his day.

> It's easier to ask for wisdom than to live it.
> The God.Life is a life shaped by wisdom.
> Wisdom isn't just for fifty- and sixty- and seventy-somethings.
> Wisdom is now.
> Chasing wisdom now creates the Kingdom.Life now.
> Wisdom makes us slow down to ask the right questions.
> Wisdom is the hardest life to live.
> Give your One.Life to wisdom.

In our culture today there are so many examples of those who, like Solomon, begin well and seem to be going in the right direction, but whose moral life comes undone. What holds life together falls apart.

I think of some "Christian" celebrities, who seem to have it all together but whose lives unravel before the watching, gawking American public. From my generation (well, a bit older), I think of Chuck Templeton, who was Canada's leading evangelist, a spiritual leader and a confidant of the young Billy Graham. But Templeton's faith began to crumble, and he ended his life ranting and raving against the Christian faith. I think of the many young people I know who begin college with a vibrant faith and big dreams and all the potential in the world, and then I hear stories later ... and it makes me think of Solomon.

We need to slow down in life and let wisdom have its way with us. If we want our big dreams to become sustainable, and if we want to end our lives well, we will need to listen to the wise. And perhaps thinking for a moment of what attracts you to Gandalf in *The Lord of the Rings* could help you refocus on the value of wisdom.

FIND A MENTOR

I was studying Proverbs chapter one and pondering the various words when an expression jumped off the page at me. Here are the words from Proverbs 1, and I want to focus on the words in italics:

> The proverbs of Solomon son of David, king of Israel:
> for gaining wisdom and instruction;
> for understanding words of insight;
> *for receiving instruction* in prudent behavior,
> doing what is right and just and fair;
> for giving prudence to those who are simple,
> knowledge and discretion to the young—
> let the wise listen and add to their learning,
> and let the discerning get guidance.
>
> *Proverbs 1:1–5*

What jumped off the page at me was the expression "for receiving instruction." As I pondered especially the word *receiving* I began to think my way around Proverbs, and then wisdom as a general idea, and then I began to think about how James, the brother of Jesus, *received* from his brother. It dawned on me that the most important posture for the one who wants to be wise is to be *receptively reverent* toward those who *are* wise.

As I read carefully through the book of James something exploded from the pages of that short letter: everyone agrees. No book sounds more like Jesus than the book of James, but he only one time quotes Jesus. James was a wise man, because he *completely absorbed* what his brother, the Messiah, had taught.

Wisdom is about
the reverence
of receiving
the wisdom of the wise.

Solomon was the fool because he stopped receiving the wisdom of God. James was wise because he received the wisdom of the Wise One. That's the wise posture of a follower of Jesus. Wise people sound like their mentors.

Let me urge you to find someone who is wise, someone who is loving, someone who is just, someone who is peaceful, and ask them if you can regularly spend time with them. Tell them they don't need to pull out a "lesson" each day or prepare anything. Ask them if you can spend time with them and do life with them once a week or once a month, so you can hear their wisdom and absorb it.

Now the hard part. I'm going to ask you not only to find a mentor and listen to a mentor, but do everything you can to do what the mentor advises you to do. The wise are those who are receptively reverent enough toward the wise that they listen and do what the wise advise.

The Kingdom.Life is the Wisdom.Life.

I learned a fresh angle on the Wisdom.Life from Andy Stanley, pastor of the Atlanta-area megachurch North Point Community Church. Andy advises that we need to learn to ask this question: "What is the wise thing to do?"[19] If you slow down enough to ask Andy's question about what you are about to do, it will illuminate everything you will ever do, and it will cast God's radiating light on all your paths. Before choosing a career, before choosing a mate, before choosing a party, before choosing friends, before having sex, before drinking, before spring break and during spring break and after spring break, before pressing on the gas pedal, before turning on the internet, before deciding which restaurant, and before choosing how to spend (or save) your money, the best question is: "What is the wise thing to do?"

I recently tried this question out. While writing this chapter and taking a break to run an errand, I drove to our local post office to send off two small packages. On the way there, I drove by a small deli that makes the world's best pastrami sandwich, Burt's Deli. As I drove by on my way to the post office, my mouth watered for that sumptuous pastrami with a pickle hopped-up with garlic, and (being that I'm overweight) I asked myself Andy Stanley's Best Question Ever: "What's the wise thing to do?"

I knew I would be coming back by Burt's Deli on the way home, so I had some time to decide. (Can you guess what I did?) That question, whether we do what is wise or not, is the way to approach all of our decisions, and it alone can keep us grounded — unlike Solomon — in living the Kingdom.Life dream of Jesus.

JESUS

Jesus was the Wise One, and so what I'd like to do is suggest elements in Jesus' own life and teachings that can help us orient our lives toward wisdom. From a multitude of things we could say, I have isolated seven elements of Jesus' wisdom and want to sketch them briefly now:

#1: Orient each day toward God.

Jesus grew up listening to a famous, famous line from Solomon: "The fear of the Lord is the beginning of wisdom" (Proverbs 9:10). The word *fear* does not suggest cowering or cringing or buckling or breaking down, though some parents or preachers might try to force a decision in their favor by attempting to create that kind of fear. No, this fear means "awe." The sort of thing you may sense when you see the Grand Canyon or brush up against some artistic scene where rich colors and grand shapes combine to send a shaft of glory into the depths of your soul. To fear God is to begin and end your day, and every moment between, with a consciousness of living with and before God. Living before God is living with an awareness that someday we all will give an account to God of what we have done and who we have been. Awe of God transforms ordinary life into the Wisdom.Life.

#2: Ask the "good question" all day long until it becomes habit.

Ambition and primal desires, these are the two problems we all face. Ambition prompts us to pursue what we want before anyone else, and primal desires prompt us to pursue pleasure. (We'll talk about sex later.) A wise person stops, thinks, ponders, and probes into her conscience and then asks: "Is this the wise thing to do?" Jesus, who was wisdom itself, did what was good and right and kind and just and holy and loving. We can wrap all those words into one burrito and sum them up with the word *good*. If we ask ourselves the right question, we will do what is good.

#3: The daily leads to the dream.

Back to the importance of our dreams. Sometimes we get to living for our dreams so much—like the person we want to marry who is a long shot plus four, like the job that makes millions, like the house that overlooks Malibu Bay, or like the challenge of teaching inner-city kids—that we forget dreams flow out of what we do daily. Jesus' dream was the Kingdom.Life, and his dream was for the whole world. That's a big dream.

How did he go about his big kingdom dream? Did he march off to Jerusalem and say, "I want this throne!" Did he get in a big boat and head off to Rome and say to Caesar, "There is no Caesar but me!" No. That was how Solomon pursued things—he wanted everything now. Jesus' approach, wisely, was to take one step at a time, and it began in Nazareth and shifted over to the Sea of Galilee a few miles and then he gathered disciples. He helped and he healed; he taught and he mentored; he listened and he observed; he did kingdom living daily. One day at a time.

Andy Stanley expresses this principle in these words: "There is a cumulative value to investing small amounts of time in certain activities over a long period."[20]

My way of saying this: Wise daily living will lead to the dream God has written into our hearts. If you neglect your daily assignments, if you fail to show up for work each day, if you fail to spend time with the one (or ones) you love, if you fail to do the ordinary task in the right way, you will get what you deserve and it won't always be good. But if you do the little wise thing daily, you will achieve the dream your life was designed to accomplish.

It works both ways:
Focus on the daily instead of the dream, but . . .
Let the dream shape what you do daily.

#4: What you want to do over there begins here.

This is a variant of number three. I begin with Jesus. What Jesus really wanted was to rule as God's Messiah on the throne. The Thief understood this and that is why he offered Jesus the temple and the world in the temptations of Jesus right after his baptism. Jesus' dream meant a throne in Jerusalem and then one in Rome. But observe where Jesus began. Jesus started in a next-to-nowhere place. There's a saying I once heard about North Dakota that I want to apply to Jesus' world: Galilee wasn't the end of the earth but you could see it from there. That's where Jesus began.

So many people have big dreams but don't realize something profoundly wise and simple:

> If you can't get the job done at home
> or in your neighborhood
> or in your dorm
> or with the folks you work with,
> Then you won't do it
> "over there" or
> "out there" or
> "in the big bad world" either.

Quite often I have students who tell me they want to pastor. If I know them and have time to build a relationship, I usually end up responding with this: If you want to pastor a church, tell me about the people you are pastoring now.

The point is simple. You don't become a pastor because some church hires you. You become a pastor because you are gifted to pastor. Some people want to pastor great big churches but show no signs of being able to pastor their children or their neighbors or the people they know well. (Or can't even get along with their closest "friends.")

Jesus started a revolution by gathering around him his personal family and local friends, and it grew from the small to the big. The wise thing to do is begin now with where you are and let that dream shape everyday living where you are. I suspect Jesus told the parable of the mustard seed — how it grew from a small seed into a bushy tree — because he knew the importance of doing little things well.

#5: Everyday people are to be everyday neighbors.

Who is in your dream? For Jesus, the ordinary folks of his day were part of his dream. I'm convinced many people begin using others around them because their ambitions and primal yearnings lead them to a future that is far off. Instead of being kind to the lady at the grocery store, instead of learning the neighbor's name, instead of treating a family member as a friend, or instead of seeing the one you work with as your companion, you may be tempted to live for a future with a group of imaginary people who neither exist now nor will exist then.

Everyday people became everyday neighbors to Jesus, because he loved every person he met. It is so easy to pass by those in our immediate circle (family, friends, neighbors) in order to show compassion to those in Africa or Southeast Asia or the inner city. But Jesus treated *everyone* as a neighbor. The wise thing is to see every person as someone loved by God, and that changes everyday people into your everyday neighbors. This is what Jesus' famous parable of the good Samaritan is all about. The question being asked in that parable is: "Who is my neighbor?" Jesus reframed it by asking, "Who's in your daily life?" That's your neighbor. Give your One.Life to your neighbor.

#6: Discover who you are by loving others.

The Golden Rule, were we to live by it, would create the Kingdom. Life and the Justice.Life and the Peace.Life in fifteen minutes. At the time of Jesus there was a debate about how to find what was most central to the Torah, the law of Moses. A story is told of a Gentile's quest to become a Jewish proselyte. So he went to a famous rabbi named Shammai and said, "Make me a proselyte on the condition that you teach me the whole Torah while I stand on one foot." Shammai, known for being strict, was repulsed by the man's arrogance and drove him away.

So the student went to the more liberal-minded Hillel with the same request. Hillel responded: "What is hateful to you, do not do to your neighbor."[21] That's Hillel's version of what Jesus said more positively: "Do to others what you want done to you." We call it the Golden Rule, and it is closely tied to what I call the Jesus Creed of loving God and loving others.

What life teaches us — if we are wise — is that by loving others we find ourselves, by giving ourselves to others we receive soul-shaping life, and by serving others we find ourselves at our deepest core. But if we think "me, me, me," we diminish ourselves, we shrink our soul, and we find ourselves lonely in the midst of millions. That's the life Solomon lived and it is unsustainable, both personally and globally. Jesus lived what one European theologian called "pro-existence." That is, he lived *for* others and it was living *for* others that brought the Kingdom.Life. In relating to others we find ourselves; in hiding ourselves from others, we lose ourselves.

C. S. Lewis once reminded his listeners and readers that forgiveness was a lovely idea until you had someone or something to forgive.[22] The same applies to loving others. Loving others is a great idea until the someone you are to love is a someone you don't like. The Wisdom.Life is shaped by loving others—all others, including the someones you don't like.

#7: Enemies can be loved easier than conquered.

Jesus extended love even to his enemies. Wisdom is known for seeing the hand of God in ordinary events in this world and in observing what today we call the laws of nature. Revolutionary words of Jesus were spoken into the pious-sounding but unsustainable conventional wisdom of his day, which was: "Love your [Jewish] neighbor and hate your [Gentile] enemy." Jesus responded to that conventional wisdom because he dreamed of a different world:

> I tell you,
> love your enemies and
> pray for those who persecute you,
> that you may be children of your Father in heaven.
> *Matthew 5:44–45*

Jesus was urging his followers to follow the way of God. If God cares for all, so ought we to do the same. If God loves all, so should God's followers. Even enemies. That meant Romans for Jesus' world.

Jesus watched the violence-oriented zealots foment hatred among both his fellow Jews and fear among the Romans in their midst. He heard stories about wars against Gentiles, and he heard dreams of tiny Israel someday regaining control of the land. But Jesus saw the way of victory and the way to gain the land and the way to bring about God's kingdom to be the way of *loving your enemies*.

An adjunct professor came to me in about the third week of classes to tell me about a student that he thought despised him. I asked him what the student's name was, because I had a suspicion. His answer: "I can't remember."

So here's what I said to him: "First, learn the student's name. Second, every time he comes into class, greet him by name. Third, before or after the next class make it a point to ask him about himself and learn what he likes."

In one week he told me he no longer had troubles with this student. In fact, he admitted, "I've gotten to where I like him and I know he likes me."

The way to make friends of your enemies is to love them and to pray for them. The way to keep them your enemies is to avoid learning their names and to avoid getting to know them. But if we pray for them, we will transform them from enemies into friends.

Jesus did the wise thing when he told his followers to love their enemies and sacrifice the temporary, unsustainable thrill of hatred on the altar of enemy-love. I can't think of a more profound illustration of the wisdom of Jesus.

IF YOU COULD HAVE ANYTHING YOU WANTED ...

There is so much more to be said, but it is probably not necessary here to sketch all of Jesus' wisdom. The real point here is to ask this question:

Is wisdom part of your dream?

Is the Kingdom.Life for you a Wisdom.Life?

There's so much, and so much good, about Jesus' Kingdom.Life, but you may be wondering how such a life is even possible. Our next chapter will examine the power of God available to use to live the Kingdom.Life.

Some of you may still be wondering what I ate for lunch that day. I asked myself the Best Question Ever three different times as I experienced the mouth-watering expectations of a pastrami sandwich ...

and I drove right by good ol' Burt's Deli and did the wiser thing: I ate a turkey sandwich at home. (No pickle either!)

One more time, our question:

According to Jesus, what is a Christian?

A Christian is one who follows Jesus by devoting her or his One.Life to the kingdom of God, fired by Jesus' own imagination, to a life of loving God and loving others, and to a society shaped by justice, especially for those who have been marginalized, to peace, and to a life devoted to acquiring wisdom.

This, I believe, sketches what Jesus thought a disciple was. Accepting Christ gets it all going, and Bible reading and prayer and church attendance are the *means,* but the goal of all of this is to follow Jesus. Following Jesus is about these elements:

Kingdom
Love
Justice
Peace
Wisdom

Interlude

When I gave my life to Jesus in high school, way back in the Fall of 1971, one of the first books I read was about how to live the Christian life. That book told me how to pray and how to read the Bible and how to live a disciplined life and how to avoid temptation and how to receive guidance and how to participate in a local church and how to serve God and how to evangelize. I drank everything up in that book, and I learned from it immensely, and I remain grateful for that book. I still have it and can see my high school underlining (with a ruler) and my marginal notes.

What surprises me about that book to this day is how little it had to do with the themes we have already sketched: kingdom, justice, love, peace, and wisdom. I've often asked myself why so many frame the Christian life in a way that has so little to do with the central themes of Jesus' own teachings and so few let Jesus' kingdom dream shape what it means to be a follower of Jesus. Sometimes I think the essence of the Christian life and the definition of a follower of Jesus are not the same for a lot of people.

I believe one reason why we frame things in a way that has so little to do with Jesus' teaching is so we can tick off the things we do well. For instance, I'm pretty good at Bible reading, so let's make that one of the central elements of following Jesus. (Never mind that Jesus lived in a world where only ten percent of the adults could read and where almost no one owned a Bible and where personal Bible reading hardly even existed.) Bible reading joins other things like prayer and attending church because these are *observable behaviors*. If they are observable, we can tick them off and pat ourselves on the back and say, "What a good girl am I!"

Yes, I believe in these things, but I believe these are a means to prompt us to be more just, more peaceful, more loving, and wiser — in other words, prayer and Bible study are designed by God to guide us into kingdom living and kingdom living is about a society — other people — shaped by God's dream for us.

So, let me change this discussion. How are you doing when it comes to Jesus' kingdom dream? How are you doing when it comes to justice? To peace? To love? To wisdom?

These are the central ideas of Jesus' kingdom dream, and they are so big and so deep ideas that we can never stop to congratulate ourselves. Instead, this kingdom dream of Jesus is so deep and compelling we are drawn into it so that we give our One.Life to it and for it.

And God's power is with us to make it happen.

CHAPTER 8

CHURCH.LIFE

For some this may be the hardest chapter to stomach.

The New Testament begins with four Gospels that tell the story of Jesus. Read these stories of Jesus through, and you are led to what comes next, the fifth book of the New Testament, which is the Acts of the Apostles. The Acts of the Apostles begins with a magnificent event called Pentecost. Someone long ago decided we'd call this book the Acts *of the Apostles* (Peter and Paul), but it would be more accurate to call it the Acts *of the Holy Spirit, Beginning at Pentecost.*

This has to be emphasized, because today too many of us emphasize kingdom but ignore the Holy Spirit and Pentecost and church — as if kingdom meant nothing more than justice and peace and love in the world (or in their country or in their state or in their local village). But that is not what Jesus means. Those terms might indicate little more than Western democratic liberalism. Now, I like Western democratic liberalism, but Jesus did not come to establish Western democratic liberalism.

One of my favorite kingdom preachers is Minneapolis pastor of Sanctuary Covenant Church, Efrem Smith. Recently I heard him make this set of connections:

> We can't arrive at the beloved community
> until we arrive at the beloved church,
> and we can't arrive at the beloved church
> until we find the beloved life —
> the life of God's love for us in Christ,

and that is visibly seen in Jesus' giving his life for us.
Life of God, church of God, and the community of God.[23]

Some people want the community of God without the Church
and life of God. One more time now: The story of the New Testament leads us from the kingdom dream of Jesus in the Gospels to
God's Spirit-created church community in the Acts of the Apostles.

There's more. Anyone who reads the Gospels through and ends
up in Acts 2 observes one thing immediately: Peter was completely
transformed. The message here is so vitally important. God's dream
is the kingdom, that's already clear. But what is not always clear
is that *God's kingdom happens when human beings are empowered
by God's Spirit to do God's kingdom work in the shape of a new
community.*

That is, when Pentecost happens, the Spirit of God ...
Transforms human abilities
and
Transcends human inabilities
so
Transformed people can participate
In God's kingdom community
In the here and now.

Something transforming and transcending happens immediately
when you cross the threshold from the Gospels into that fifth book.
Jesus' followers become the church community that acts like kingdom community. Why? The Spirit of God is present. The Gospels
lead to the Acts, because the kingdom dream of Jesus forms Spirit-
transforming communities.

Where the Spirit is, there is community.
Where there is community, there is Spirit.

The Spirit whispers *community* everywhere the Spirit goes. Where
there is community, there is Spirit. Where there is no community,
there is no Spirit. The Spirit brings love, justice, and peace—for all
in the community. In fact, it takes God's Spirit to create community
because we, no matter how hard we try, are unloving, unjust, and
unpeaceful. We need the Spirit to live in community.

Before we take another step we have to face an issue. Jesus and the earliest followers were big on the Holy Spirit. They weren't weird and they weren't wandering ecstatics and they weren't mystical introverts. But they believed God both visited them in fresh power and indwelled them through the Holy Spirit. Some have ignored the Spirit so much that Francis Chan wrote a book called *The Forgotten God* to call our attention once again to the Holy Spirit.[24] Perhaps we can remind ourselves again of what happens when Pentecost happens: Community emerges because the Spirit is designed to draw us to God and to one another into a fellowship and community.

Some are afraid to ask God's Spirit to come down to empower us and fill us, but Francis Chan thinks the question is actually deeper: "The flip side of fearing that God won't show up is fearing that he *will*." And if the Spirit comes, community will come.

Please don't mistake what I'm saying. We are not talking about church as many have experienced it. We are not necessarily talking about denominations or church buildings or catechism classes or priests or organs or parking lots or anything like that. Some churches, in fact, are like shopping malls: people park their nice cars, enter the building, get what they want, get back in the car and go out to eat. But that's not community (and it's really not church either). The word we are using is *community*, and we dare not confuse community-less church or Christianity or religion or Christendom with what the Spirit creates. The Spirit creates community that makes church what the kingdom wants church to be. So, when I say "Church.Life" I mean that kind of community, but it is in a church where that community forms.

At the very core of the kingdom dream of Jesus there is a focus on God's society, the Church. The dream of Jesus never lets anyone dwell in solitude; the dream of Jesus never creates individualism. The dream of Jesus always creates kingdom community. Perhaps you had the community dream crushed from you by bad experiences or legalism or friendship cliques or weird, annoying people. It is just as likely that your community dream was crushed by your church being quintessentially boring. I experience these problems myself. To be honest, I have helped create that kind of community-less church.

I have no desire to pretend the problems with churches are not real. But I'm asking you to take a good hard look at what Jesus (and his earliest followers) thought community was, and then to ask yourself if you might be interested in that kind of dream.

Before we go any further, a word of caution: Community is like peace in that it is a result instead of an action. Peace results from acts of justice and behaviors of love. Community also emerges out of loving behaviors—like compassion and an embrace and forgiveness—and out of acts of justice. Once again, many people say they want a genuine community but are not willing to lay down their lives in the pain of genuine relational struggle so that community will emerge as it did when Pentecost first happened. Which leads to this question:

WHAT IS THE CHURCH.LIFE?

Each of the four Gospels prepares us for a Jewish festival called Pentecost. On the day of Pentecost, the Spirit of God came rushing down like Zeus from Mt. Olympus and swarmed that little community of Jesus' followers who believed Jesus' dream. They all began to speak in "tongues," which means they lost control of their tongues and God used their tongues to declare the wonders of God. This may weird you out as much as it weirded out those who saw the spectacle. Regardless of your weird meter on this one, the big issue for us is what happened soon after that event. You can find the report at the very end of the second chapter of the Acts of the Apostles, one of my favorite passages in the whole Bible:

> They devoted themselves to the apostles' teaching and to fellowship, to the breaking of bread and to prayer. Everyone was filled with awe at the many wonders and signs performed by the apostles. All the believers were together and had everything in common. They sold property and possessions to give to anyone who had need. Every day they continued to meet together in the temple courts. They broke bread in their homes and ate together with glad and sincere hearts, praising God and enjoying the favor of all the people. And the Lord added to their number daily those who were being saved.
>
> *Acts 2:42–47*

This is what community is and this is what church is and this is why we should be able to say "community" and mean "church." This is what it looks like when the Spirit overcomes a group of people. Pentecost can happen. This is what love, justice, and peace look like. Now the most important observation: This is the kind of kingdom society Jesus had in mind.

One of my former students, Amanda, and one of the finest I've had in my fifteen years at North Park University, is now in a very successful career. She finished off college with a flourish, went on to graduate school, and now has a dream job.

Amanda recently told me she gave up on church because she can't find anything about Sunday morning that (1) looks like what Jesus was all about or (2) holds her interest anymore. She can't think that Jesus' mission was to create one-hour services where pastors preach for forty minutes while passive parishioners sit (on hard seats) and take it all in as if it is designed for them. She can't think that spending thousands of dollars on pretty buildings is what Jesus thought should be done with the funds of his followers. She can't think Jesus would want God's called servants to spend their entire week gearing up for a one-hour performance.

She's right.

What many churches offer is not what you want to give your One.Life for. Where did we get the idea that church is a one-hour Sunday morning service at 11:00 a.m.? Not from Jesus, not from his dream parables, and not from his vision of the Kingdom.Life.

Many today are looking for connectedness in a common life, and many are willing to devote their One.Life to that kind of society, but what they are finding at that weekly gathering is a group of folks gathered but disconnected. The tragedy is that it doesn't have to be this way. Something can be done about it. It begins if we will return to the community vision of the earliest followers of Jesus and let Pentecost happen all over again. Notice what we see in this earliest of Christian communities, a life that can only be called Church.Life:

Life lived with others, regardless of who they are
Life shaped by the teachings of Jesus through his apostles
Life experienced by eating with one another

Life swarmed by prayer
Life carried away in awe of what God was doing
Life shared economically and materially
Life welcomed by outsiders
Life expanded
Life unleashed

I think if more people were finding these things at the local church, they'd pitch in and say, "This is what Life-to-the-Full looks like and I want some of it!" I would characterize the community life of Pentecost with these words:

Friendship
Teaching the faith
Common meals
Spirituality
Worship
Holistic care for one another
Integrity
Growth

What is the alternative?

Life lived alone and unsatisfied
Life shaped by someone or something else other than Jesus
Life experienced by dining alone
Life with thick spaces between you and God
Life noted by pursuing more and more stuff
Life shaped by: "What's mine is mine!"
Life unnoticed by others
Life stunted by "groupishness" and cliques
Life protected

As I wrote these last two paragraphs there was an ongoing conversation on my blog about a post called "iGens 10." We are conversing about Jean Twenge's powerful description of her own generation in her book *Generation Me*. A professor and researcher at San Diego State University, Twenge observes social generation trends. At the time of her research, she discovered that the current generation of eighteen-to thirty-five-year-olds are marked more and more by anxiety and depression. Her explanation? There is too much of an expectation for iGens to stand alone. That is, they are taught to be independent, think independently, become financially independent, and make it on their own. She also observes that we are wired to love others and to need others.[25]

A wise pastor near a major university, Jim Martin, just wrote a comment on the blog with these words:

> I really believe that the next generation is looking for genuine fellowship. Between an individual person and another. In families. In clusters of people. For many of them, fellowship is not something lost. Rather, it has never existed in their experience. For many of them, it may have never existed in their family of origin nor have they even been able to observe it in families of their peers.
>
> One challenge for churches is going to be to really see/care about this generation and be willing to adjust, mentor, and provide both models and the experience of some kind of authentic fellowship.

The irony grips me hard. What the Church is designed to be — a community, a society. etc. — is what the Church is not. What the Church needs to offer the next generation is precisely what it is not: a fellowship. What the next generation needs more than to stand alone is to stand with others, to experience fellowship, and it makes me ask if the Church is up for the challenge. The same generation that produced iGens who crave fellowship is the same generation directing the Church.

Somewhere along the line kingdom became personal spirituality and Sunday gatherings became services. Somewhere along the line the Church became a place where individuals could gather on Sunday for one hour and feed their precious souls. Somewhere along the line we converted Jesus' kingdom dream into a personal-spirituality dream. Somewhere along the line kingdom ceased being *society* and became *spirituality*. The impact is devastating for a generation that needs fellowship more than any generation in history. We are standing now, as individuals, at the onset of the twenty-first century, looking at beautiful buildings with a wonderful history, but, if we are honest, we are also wondering if the twenty-second century will even know who we are and what churches were designed to accomplish.

In the summer of 2008, Kris and I visited Pompeii in Italy, the site of one of the most magnificent ruins in the world. Pompeii was destroyed when Mount Vesuvius exploded, burying the entire city and killing thousands and thousands of unsuspecting people. One of the most remarkable features of Pompeii is that it lay unnoticed for nearly 1,700 years. A village named La Civita had grown up on and over Pompeii. No one even noticed until in the late eighteenth century someone found some ruins. Someone else wondered if the ruins might have come from Pompeii. Someone else said, "Let's figure this out."

Today you can wander through those magnificent ruins for hours (and we did for almost five hours). I wonder if the twenty-second century won't walk all over the Church-ianity of our day and build its sites over the tops of our megachurches. And I wonder if some later generation will be the ones who discover the non-community form of life that used to be called "church." I really do wonder.

It could happen if the Church today doesn't wake up to the cry for fellowship and the mission to be community. The current generation yearns for this. In fact, we all yearn for it—but many of us have simply given up or caved in and settled for the Thin.Life or the Personal.Life.

But there is hope because we can enter into the kingdom dream of Jesus all over again by asking once again for the Spirit of Pentecost to fill us, to baptize us, to swarm us, and to revolutionize us so that we live as that early fellowship of Jesus followers lived. The Church.Life begins when we turn our minds, our hearts, and our hands toward God and ask God to flood us with the Spirit of God. Is that your prayer?

WHAT IS A CHRISTIAN?

A Christian is one who follows Jesus by devoting his or her One.Life to the kingdom of God, fired by Jesus' own imagination, to a life of loving God and loving others, and to a society shaped by justice, especially for those who have been marginalized, to peace, and to a life devoted to acquiring wisdom in the context of a local church. This life can only be discovered by being empowered by God's Spirit.

So how do we get this Kingdom.Life?

Interlude

I've been thinking of asking this question for a few chapters, so maybe I shouldn't wait any longer: Why is it so easy to work for kingdom purposes but ignore your local church? Why do we see kingdom work in such idealistic terms but look down our noses at our local churches? Do you think Jesus ignored the local in order to chase the kingdom? Or did he want us to be inspired to enter into the imagined life of his parables and then bring that back to the ordinary relations of our ordinary world?

This division between church and kingdom needs to be examined afresh. What Jesus meant by kingdom was the society where God's will is done. But any reading of the Gospels will show that he knew that the kingdom dream wouldn't happen all at once in a perfect and sudden way. He knew it meant hard work, struggles, and interpersonal conflict with real people in our own neighborhoods. He knew his own followers weren't perfect and their society wasn't living up to the ideal. His closest follower denied him; his specially chosen apostles were power-hungry and reputation-grubbing. Yet, those were his people and the ones he chose to concentrate all of his attentions on.

Local churches aren't perfect, and if you are looking for the perfect local church, you won't find it. But here's something I've learned: Local churches reflect the realities of real humans who participate in kingdom living in a world broken by sin and systemic evil. Kingdom life is designed to take root in local communities, and it is the vision of Jesus for you and me to make our local community of faith our primary launching place for kingdom-dream living. Neither your local community nor mine will be the perfect one. Our challenge is to settle in and strive for the kingdom dream—empowered by God's Spirit—from the local community into the global village. It's much harder but it's the real world.

I wonder if the African word from a previous chapter, *Ubuntu*, shows us something here too. What makes *Ubuntu* so notable is the stubborn commitment of Africans to dwell with one another, to work with one another, and to be committed to one another even when they fall short of their own *Ubuntu* ideals.

So, Jesus' kingdom dream is meant for this world and is meant for folks like you and me. We fall short of our own ideals, and we dwell with others who fall short. Perhaps the commitment of "short-of-ideals" people to one another is the very heart of what Jesus means by kingdom living in the here and now. Which has taught me this: I owe my primary commitment to my local church, not because it is what I want and not because it is the ideal place, but because the only way for Jesus' dream kingdom to take root is when local people commit to one another to strive with one another for a just, loving, peaceful, and wise society, beginning at home, with friends, and at their local community of faith.

CHAPTER 9

COMMITTED LIFE

Jesus was a zealot. Zealotry has its advantages when it is directed at the right object. Jesus was a *moral* zealot. He was an extremist, and I'd like you to consider the challenges he gave to his followers. The first thing I want to ask you, though, is to turn your gaze from the Church and turn away from everyone you know who calls himself or herself a Christian. I want you to do what Craig Keener, a devout follower of Jesus, once had to learn when he converted from atheism to Jesus. When he was an atheist, he said one of his nonscientific reasons for not following Jesus was that 80 percent of the people in his country claimed to be Jesus' followers, yet most of them apparently lived as if it made no difference for their lives.

Craig knew of some genuine followers of Jesus but, after studying the Gospels carefully, he came to this conclusion: "I reasoned that if I believed that there was truly a being to whom I owed my existence and who alone determined my eternal destiny, I would serve that being unreservedly." He reasoned further: "If [these] Christians did not really believe in Jesus, there was surely no reason for myself to do so."[26]

Just read these words and imagine listening to them, believing them, and imagining what life would be like if you did them just as he said. First, three separate people draw out of Jesus (in bold) a response that summons them to follow him unreservedly:

> As they were walking along the road, a man said to him, "I will follow you wherever you go." Jesus replied, "Foxes have holes and birds have nests, but the Son of Man has no place to lay his head."

He said to another man, "Follow me." But he replied, "Lord, first let me go and bury my father." Jesus said to him, "Let the dead bury their own dead, but you go and proclaim the kingdom of God."

Still another said, "I will follow you, Lord; but first let me go back and say good-by to my family." Jesus replied, "No one who puts a hand to the plow and looks back is fit for service in the kingdom of God."

Luke 9:57–62

These sayings of Jesus summon his listeners to the kingdom commitment, and an inner core of that commitment is holy indifference about what others think and about what others say and about what others do to you because of your kingdom commitment. Jesus believed in the Committed.Life.

Jesus' kingdom commitment turned everything upside down, including what we gain and buy and wear, and what we do with what we have and even how much we have:

Sell your possessions and give to the poor. Provide purses for yourselves that will not wear out, a treasure in heaven that will never fail, where no thief comes near and no moth destroys.

Luke 12:33

In the same way, those of you who do not give up everything you have cannot be my disciples.

Luke 14:33

And why do you worry about clothes? See how the flowers of the field grow. They do not labor or spin. Yet I tell you that not even Solomon in all his splendor was dressed like one of these. If that is how God clothes the grass of the field, which is here today and tomorrow is thrown into the fire, will he not much more clothe you — you of little faith?

Matthew 6:28–30

George Washington, our nation's first president, made an observation about what to wear: "Play not the peacock, looking every where about you, to see if you be well deck't, if your shoes fit well, if your stockings sit neatly, and clothes handsomely."[27] Jesus digs even deeper than Washington's concern with pomposity and pride.

Jesus digs into the inner chambers of the heart. The single-most glaring contradiction between Jesus' life and our lives today—and I'm speaking to the Western-world Christian—pertains to money and possessions. Jim Wallis captures it well when he says, "Because of our fascination with wealth, our economy has been sustained by buying things we don't need, with money that we don't have." And someone has added this: "to impress people we don't like with things that don't last." As seminary students Jim and friends examined the Bible to find every reference to the poor—and they found more than two thousand. In fact, they concluded one of every sixteen verses was about the poor. Then a zealous friend decided to cut out every Bible verse about the poor to see what the Bible would look like. As he tells the story, "that old Bible literally was in shreds. It wouldn't hold together. It was a Bible full of holes."[28]

Recently I read the story of Andrea Jaeger, who rose as a teenager to be the number two tennis player in the world.[29] But Andrea Jaeger, though earning enough money to be set in opulence for life, was unsatisfied because of the kingdom call to compassion for kids with cancer. Today Andrea Jaeger is an Episcopal nun devoted to caring for suffering children. I suspect Andrea's choices have been closer to what Jesus had in mind than the mild "cutting back" and "giving" we find among Western Christians, and I say this to myself as much as to all of us.

What about these words from Matthew's fifth chapter? Jesus goes right to the heart of morality:

> For I tell you that unless your righteousness surpasses that of the Pharisees and the teachers of the law, you will certainly not enter the kingdom of heaven.
>
> *Matthew 5:20*

Jesus is a moral zealot; he's relentless; he expects his followers to sell out to him and for him and to give him everything, including the deepest of passions. He goes to the heart of anger and tells his disciples they are to forgive and to work for reconciliation:

> You have heard that it was said to the people long ago, 'You shall not murder, and anyone who murders will be subject to judgment.' But I tell you that **anyone who is angry with a brother or sister will be subject to judgment. Again, anyone who says to a brother or sister, '*Raca*,' is answerable to the Sanhedrin. And anyone who says, 'You fool!' will be in danger of the fire of hell.**
>
> *Matthew 5:21–22*

Forgiveness is hard, but I think Jesus expects his followers to work at it. Few have lived the pains and joys of forgiveness like the Rwandans, who, after experiencing the horror of genocide—some 800,000 Tutsi were murdered—have tried to put their society back together through a process called *Gacaca*, their ancient form of justice. Under the shade of their wild fig trees (*umuvumu*), trusted elders and women and men meet to hear cases—and they had to do this because it would have taken 200 years to hear the cases of the murderers and slaughterers in their legal courts. The law moved into the hands of the people, and justice is at stake. But forgiveness and grace, administered under the *umuvumu* trees, are creating a new day for Rwanda.

For an example drawn from thousands that are now being told, Gahigi was a Tutsi pastor who lost all but eight of the 150 members of his Tutsi family.[30] He survived by escaping to a refugee camp in Burundi. Healing over time and through months of painful prayer, Gahigi knew he was called to speak to those imprisoned for heinous crimes, some of whom had murdered those he loved. After he was done speaking to the prisoners one time, a prisoner approached him and said, "Have mercy, have mercy." Then the prisoner confessed to Gahigi: "I spent many sleepless nights over you. I searched for you so I could kill you. But have mercy on me and forgive me."

What's it like to face a murderer of your own flesh and blood? What's it like to face such a person who asks for grace and forgiveness? What does one say and do? Gahigi, tested to the deepest fabric of his soul, embraced the man and forgave him—and unleashed a cycle of grace that is spreading slowly but perceptibly into *shalom* in Rwanda.

Neither Jesus nor anyone today is suggesting forgiveness is easy or painless, but forgiveness and reconciliation lead us straight into the kingdom dream of Jesus where love and peace and justice flow.

Jesus goes on and now directs his words to the heart of sexual desires:

> "You have heard that it was said, 'You shall not commit adultery.' But I tell you that **anyone who looks at a woman lustfully has already committed adultery with her in his heart**. If your right eye causes you to stumble, gouge it out and throw it away. It is better for you to lose one part of your body than for your whole body to be thrown into hell. And if your right hand causes you to stumble, cut it off and throw it away. It is better for you to lose one part of your body than for your whole body to go into hell."
>
> *Matthew 5:27–30*

But Jesus goes beyond holy indifference toward others and toward things and toward our desires. He zooms in his favorite—love your neighbors as yourself—and applies it directly to those farthest from one's neighbors, and surely this is one of his most radical demands:

> But I tell you, love your enemies and pray for those who persecute you.
>
> *Matthew 5:44*

G. K. Chesterton said, "The Bible tells us to love our neighbors, and also to love our enemies; probably because they are generally the same people."[31] That's witty and true, but it's also not quite what Jesus was saying: he was telling his contemporaries that the way to deal with the Roman occupation and the way to conquer was the path of love. It's easy to love Israelites; it's hard to love Romans. Jesus called his contemporaries to love both.

So Jesus sums up his demand for his followers in just one line, a line that perfectly expresses the kingdom commitment:

> **Be perfect**, therefore, as your heavenly Father is perfect.
>
> *Matthew 5:48*

Now for the hard truth: Jesus expected his followers to listen and do what he said in the Sermon on the Mount. Unfortunately, his invitation words coming at the end of the sermon are softened for so many who learned those same words in a cute little kids' song that we enacted by falling to the ground. "All fall down!" we said as we tumbled together to the ground in a bundle of laughter. But these words of Jesus are serious, serious words from a serious, serious man.

Therefore everyone who **hears these words of mine and puts them into practice** is like a wise man who built his house on the rock. The rain came down, the streams rose, and the winds blew and beat against that house; yet it did not fall, because it had its foundation on the rock.

But everyone **who hears these words of mine and does not put them into practice** is like a foolish man who built his house on sand. The rain came down, the streams rose, and the winds blew and beat against that house, and it fell with a great crash.

Matthew 7:24–27

HE CAN'T BE SERIOUS ...

Many have softened the blow of these words of Jesus. For instance, one of America's most famous world-religions experts, Huston Smith, a son of missionaries who later said, "I never met a religion I did not like," tones down Jesus' demands to this: "If you think Jesus Christ is special, in his own category of specialness, and you feel an affinity for him, and you do not harm others consciously, you can consider yourself a Christian."[32]

Do Smith's words sound like Jesus' words?

Not to me. Ask the rich young ruler; I'm sure he thought Jesus meant what he said:

Just then a man came up to Jesus and asked, "Teacher, what good thing must I do to get eternal life?"

"Why do you ask me about what is good?" Jesus replied. "There is only One who is good. **If you want to enter life, keep the commandments.**"

"**Which ones?**" he inquired.

Jesus replied, "'You shall not murder, you shall not commit adultery, you shall not steal, you shall not give false testimony, honor your father and mother,' and 'love your neighbor as yourself.'"

"All these I have kept," the young man said. "**What do I still lack?**"

Jesus answered, "If you want to be perfect, go, sell your possessions and give to the poor, and you will have treasure in heaven. Then come, follow me."

When the young man heard this, he went away sad, because he had great wealth.

Matthew 19:16–22

So we ask again, can Jesus be serious? I think he is. Pick up Matthew's gospel, open it up to chapter five and start reading for yourself. You tell me if Jesus is dead serious or not. (He is.)

He summoned people to do what he said.
He didn't summon people to do what he said *perfectly.*
He summoned people to follow him.
He didn't summon people to follow him *perfectly.*

Well, yes, I take that back. He did summon them to perfection, but the pattern of the best disciples, the twelve apostles, was that they followed him but did not follow him perfectly. When they messed up, Jesus rebuked them, told them to knock it off, and summoned them back to following him. Jesus' relationship with the apostles proves that he didn't demand sinless perfection. Instead, he demanded that his followers follow him. He expected them to follow him because he believed followers of Jesus really do follow Jesus.

One way of putting this is that Jesus wanted perfect commitment but knew that he would not get perfection from us. Perfect commitment means that we surrender who we are and all we have and all we want and all our plans to Jesus.

What Jesus meant by "be perfect" are like the words of the Grammy-winning song "Smooth," featuring Rob Thomas with Santana. In 1999, his song was number one for twelve consecutive weeks.

Give me your heart
Make it real
Or else forget about it

I can see Jesus using those very words to his disciples and especially to wannabe disciples. That's the way he was and that's how he talked because that's what he expected. Here's our problem today. Not only do we not like ultimatums, but we have too many Christians who have accepted Jesus into their hearts and who have been baptized and who have confessed their sins and who have joined the Church and who are in Bible studies and who are absolutely 100 percent convinced they are going to heaven, but who are *not* followers of Jesus.

There are many who haven't made it real. The mark of a follower of Jesus is following. The mark of a follower of Jesus is that she or he has given Jesus her or his heart. It's that simple. It's that demanding. It's that serious. Jesus was a moral zealot and he expected his followers to become moral zealots too. He wanted them to live the Committed. Life.

COWARD.LIFE

Richard Stearns is now the president of World Vision, one of the most visible Christian relief and development organizations in the world. Richard was a Christian but he admits that in his wildly successful and even opulent lifestyle he had become a "coward for God" until ...

A friend, Bill Bryce, was raising money for a top-notch seminary but had been offered a new job to raise money for World Vision. In making that decision, Bill asked Richard for his advice, and Richard thought it was a no-brainer—raising money for a dusty seminary versus raising money to save starving children was not a decision. Thirteen years later Bill, still with World Vision, which was losing its fine president, called Richard to tell him that he sensed God might be calling Richard to be the next president.

Richard laughed at him. His words: "I wasn't even interested or available. I had made it to the top, loved my job, loved my house and community, and had five young kids who attended a great Christian school, and I had no intention of uprooting them." His friend Bill pushed a little more and Richard got pushy himself, and closed the phone conversation with these memorable words: "If God wants me, He knows where to find me." After all, Richard reasoned, he was running a luxury business selling goods to the rich. But Richard Stearns faced the toughest existential challenge he'd ever met. It all came down to this self-pondering statement he had to face: "*You lack one thing, Rich. Sell your possessions and give to the poor, and you will have treasure in heaven. Then come, follow me.*"

Richard confessed: "In my own life, success, the prestige of my career, the admiration I felt from others because of it, and the financial prosperity that had come with it had become more and more important to my identity." It was a struggle because comfort and money and what Jesus called *mammon* has a way of suffocating our willingness to do what Jesus wants us to do. But World Vision knew Richard was the person for the job so they called. Richard interviewed; World Vision offered him the presidency. But Richard backed off and wobbled and gave lame excuses.

Then after a missions conference one night, Richard sat with his wife, Renée, in their kitchen when it all came crashing down on him: the needs of the children around the world and his intoxication with a career and the call of Jesus upon his life and the gospel of the kingdom that means more than fire insurance.

He broke down sobbing. God was calling. That April he accepted, in May he resigned from his business, in June he became World Vision's president, in July the movers collected his stuff from his two-hundred-year-old farmhouse on five acres, in August he was in the jungles of Uganda. He's been traveling the world for World Vision ever since.[33]

THE SUM OF IT ALL

I've been teaching for more than two decades. I've been studying the teachings of Jesus as a professional, which doesn't make me perfect or mean my ideas are better, but it does at least mean I've been at this awhile.

There are a number of words that run like water through each of those sayings we have already quoted from Jesus. We can call this set of Jesus' teachings *holiness* or *righteousness* or *discipleship* or *kingdom vision*, but what we call them is not that important.

What is important is that we have two options:

You can dismiss Jesus' morally zealous words as unrealistic.
OR
You can take his words as a summons to give yourself to Jesus.

That is, you can take these words as a summons to love God and to love Jesus and to love yourself and to love others — totally. Jesus' teachings are not a set of morals or a set of teachings or even a lofty utopian law or a religion. They are profound, provocative, utterly (at times) unthinkable and undoable challenges to get you to take a look at who it is that utters these words, to think about whether or not he's worth the effort, and a summons to give your entire self—heart, soul, mind, strength, body, and spirit—to Jesus himself.

> They are a summons to love him and to give yourself to him
> The way a lover gives her body to the one she loves
> The way a man gives his body to the woman he loves
> In every act of love you either give your heart or trade your soul
> But ...
> Jesus invites you to give yourself to him, an act of heart *and* soul

Yes, like in the lyrics of "Smooth," he invites you into two options: "Give me your heart. Make it real. Or else forget about it." Jesus is a love-me-completely zealot.

Jesus doesn't want just your talents. He doesn't want just your dreams. He doesn't want just your abilities. He doesn't want just your mind. He doesn't want just your job. He doesn't want only your grades. He doesn't want just your boyfriend or girlfriend. He doesn't want just your money. He doesn't want just your kids or your spouse. He doesn't want just your gifts.

> He wants *you*.
> He doesn't want something *from you*, he wants *you*.
> He wants your One.Life.
> He wants you to live the Committed.Life.

He isn't asking you to commit to a system or an idea or an ideal. He isn't asking you to throw yourself into a religion or a logical system. First and foremost, and without this the whole thing crumbles into a deconstructed myth, he wants you to commit yourself unreservedly to him.

If you give *yourself* to Jesus, he transforms your talents and your dreams and your abilities and your mind and your job and your grades and the relationship to the ones you love and your money and he converts them into kingdom explorations and kingdom challenges. When you give yourself to Jesus, your life becomes the Kingdom.Life. But the Kingdom.Life only happens when you give yourself (your One.Life) to Jesus, and that means also to his kingdom dream and to those who are in that kingdom dream already.

His vision becomes real very fast. When Jesus speaks to us about our total life he means our body and sex and he means our job and what we give our life to on a daily basis. So I'd like to explore with you what a kingdom vision means for two of the most common dimensions of life: our love life and our work life.

Interlude

I've never met anyone who is against peace with God and others, and I've never met anyone against justice, and I've never met anyone who is really against love. In fact, it is not a stretch to think that the kingdom dream of Jesus puts into words the deepest dream of everyone. Which leads to the double-edged question:

Why is this dream still so much about the future and
so little about what is going on now?

Let me stop what I think may be going on in the heads of many: the answer to that double-edged question is not to be sought in the faults of others. We can't stand up now and say, "It would happen if everyone in the world were like me." We can't point our fingers and say, "It's because of the Communists or the Marxists or the Democrats or the Republicans." We can't even point at our parents and say, "If only I hadn't had a cold and distant father."

I want to ask this question more directly now and I'm asking you to be deadly honest:

Why is this kingdom dream still so much about your future and
not about what is going on in your life right now?

Why aren't you realizing this dream in your life? Why do you find yourself not at peace with God and with yourself and with others? Why are you not practicing justice everywhere you go? Why are you not loving some people but loving others?

Why do you want this dream but can't find it?

Why do you crave the Kingdom.Life

but are afraid to reach out and take it?

It is too easy to ask this question and then get distracted by interesting and stimulating things in life, so I want to ask you to think about this seriously. Somehow we've got to face an all-too-real set of questions we all encounter:

Why do we want what we know is best,

what is good, what is loving,

what is peaceful, what is just

and what is wise ...

but can't find the energy, the resources, the willpower,

or the ability to live them out on a day-to-day basis?

Why are you holding back?

What are you holding back?

CHAPTER 10

SEX.LIFE

She was sitting in my office, hesitant and nervous and wondering what I would think.

■ ■ ■

She suddenly said, "My boyfriend and I have been doing something I'm embarrassed about." She hesitated some more and her face began to flush and she began to tear up. "We've been sleeping together. Everyone on campus now knows. What should I do?" I did my best not to act surprised; I did my best to approach her with the healing words of God's grace; and I did my best to let her explore her own conscience. We spent some time together; she trusted me and never saw me the same way again. One of her most powerful comments though was this: "I've ruined my reputation with some of my friends, and I will disappoint my mom so much when I tell her—but I will." Then this question: "Do you think I will ever feel like God has forgiven me?"

■ ■ ■

He was sitting in my office, trembling over what he had done.

He fumbled with some words, and then just blurted out this question: "Do you think I will lose my salvation because I had sex with my girlfriend?" I asked a question or two, as the fuller story unfolded. He had sex with his girlfriend three years earlier, as a high school junior. It violated everything he had been taught by his parents and his church; and he said it violated his own conscience. His single-time sexual activity with his girlfriend had tormented his soul and mind for three years. I was the first person he had told, and all he wanted to know was if God forgives sins of a sexual nature.

SEX AND THE KINGDOM VISION

In her mind-blowing survey of sexual behaviors on college campuses, called *Sex and the Soul*, Donna Freitas discovers two sorts of students, and the names this professor uses for them might surprise you. She's discovered both "godly" students and "secular" students. The first group fully integrates faith and their sexual behaviors — even when they don't live up to them — while the second group finds no (or almost no) connection between spirituality and sexual behaviors. The "godly" students do not believe sex is a personal decision but is instead "always religious" and it is always "other-centered."

Freitas discovered that their faith tells godly students to see things this way. The "secular" students, on the other hand, split sex and religion into two entirely separate spheres, according to Freitas. What they do sexually is "nobody else's business as long as everyone directly involved consents."[34] But it is not because the secular students are not spiritual; in fact, Freitas concluded that the secular students' spirituality simply says almost nothing about sex. For some of them, good sexual relations *are* a form of spirituality.

If you have One.Life, what do you want your love and sex life to look like when you look back on it when you are older?

Someone who follows Jesus and who gives her or his One.Life to the kingdom dream of Jesus, and that means surrendering to become a moral zealot like Jesus, asks yet another question: What does Jesus' kingdom dream — a kingdom marked by self-sacrificing love, justice, wisdom, and peace — have to say about the sexual culture of today? Where does sexuality fit into the dream kingdom of Jesus?

Besides the rather obvious point that Jesus grew up in a world marked by Torah, and a Torah that prohibited sex for anyone outside of marriage and yet showed that sex was a gift from God and therefore good, how does his dream for love, peace, wisdom, and justice impact sexual behaviors? I don't know if you've ever thought about sexual behaviors in light of Jesus' kingdom vision, but that vision has much to say about sexuality—and sexuality today is on steroids.

THREE KINDS OF SEXUAL STATISTICS

There are three kinds of statistics about the actual sexual behaviors of young (and not always) adults today.

The first kind of statistics cover the *details*.

- By the time of graduation from high school, almost 75 percent of high school students have had sex.
- Adolescent females who are sexually active between fifteen and nineteen years old will have, on average, seven different sexual partners during their lives.
- Sixteen percent of high school students have had four or more sexual partners.
- About 70 percent of college students have had sex with at least one partner in the last year.
- Nearly 50 percent of college students have had oral sex in the last thirty days.
- Between 10 percent (females) and 17 percent (males) of college students have had three or more partners in the last year.

A second kind of statistics concern *attitudes and experiences*, and this evidence should deeply concern the follower of Jesus.

Only one-third of the females report that they really wanted to have sex the first time they had sex. (There's more here than just hesitancy about sex; many of these women admit to coercion and unwillingness to do what they did.)

"While two out of three young men said it was better to get married than go through life single, *fewer than half of the young women felt that way*"—so reports Laura Sessions Stepp who has become America's leading journalist on the sexual behaviors of young women. The subtitle of her book *Unhooked* reveals a powerful undercurrent in the hook-up culture: *How Young Women Pursue Sex, Delay Love and Lose at Both*.[35]

Sessions Stepp also tells us that in one study of 555 undergrads, almost four out of five had hooked up and that "half said they started their evenings planning to have some form of sex, with no particular person in mind."[36]

Many who engage in sexual behaviors this way walk home that night, or the next morning, absorbed with a sense of shame.

Erwin McManus, pastor at Los Angeles's Mosaic, captures this thought perfectly: "There is no such thing as free sex. It always comes at a cost. With it, either you give your heart, or you give your soul." That is, "you can have sex without giving love, but you can't have sex without giving a part of yourself."[37]

The results—the statistics above—show that many, if not most, of young adults dabbling in casual sex are profoundly dissatisfied with it, dissatisfied enough that they are calling into question the single most important institution in society: marriage.

The third and most important statistic in all of this though has to do with *the nature of the relationship*:

Almost none of these students is in a serious, long-term relationship with the one with whom they are engaging in sexual activities.

Few today would be surprised to hear that sex has found a way to break itself free from faith, but evidence now shows that sex has also lost its moorings to a serious relationship. Sex has become getting "hooked up" with those who are (relationally) "unhooked from" a serious relationship.

It is too easy to pull the heavy hammer out on this one and pound away with expressions like "it's wrong" or "purity matters" or "sex is for marriage"—all of which Jesus would have inherited from his parents and read in his Torah and absorbed in his culture. But evidence shows that the "it's wrong" strategy is not working, and so we want to go deeper and ask if words like *kingdom* and *justice* and *love* and *righteousness* and *wisdom* address these pervasive sexual behaviors today.

What kind of sexual relationships do you want in the One.Life you've got?

BEHAVIORS OF LOVE

One day after a session of my class Women, the Bible, and the Church— a class that explores both what the Bible says about women and a theology of relationships—a young woman asked me if she could talk to me. In less than five minutes she said these things: "This class comes at the perfect time for me. I've been living with my boyfriend for a year. I never wanted to but he insisted, and a few weeks back he got mad and left. I've not seen him since. I need this class to think again about who I am and what it means to love a man. Thanks."

"I'm glad you are taking this class," I said.

And she walked away. It made me head back to my office pondering what my students might be going through—most of them in silence.

After interviewing scads of young women who opened up the closets of their hooking-up practices to her, Laura Sessions Stepp spoke of the damage this does to young women: "A girl can tuck a Trojan in her purse on Saturday night, but there is no such device to protect her heart."[38]

In other words, there's more to sex than the body. Sex implicates the emotions. Because there is no prophylactic for the heart, many today suppress the emotions involved in a genuine relationship. A professor of health education at Indiana University asks this question: "Hooking up is purposely uncaring. If they turn off the emotional spigot during this time, what will happen to them as older adults?"[39]

Listen to these words of a young woman: "You're supposed to know what to do and how to do it and how to feel during and afterward. You learn to turn everything off except your body and make yourself emotionally invulnerable."[40]

And yet another woman expresses how she has learned to steel herself against the pain, but she makes her point in a question that reveals the self-inflicted wounds of our sexual culture: "Does that part of us that seeks connection eventually start to break down when we no longer associate sex with love?"[41]

After interviewing college students who had been involved in sex with partners to whom they were not committed, Donna Freitas observes, "After a few years of living in the environment they felt exhausted, spent, emptied by the pressure to participate in encounters that left them unfulfilled."[42]

While some emerging adults do (rarely) report general sexual and emotional happiness after sex with uncommitted partners, studies show that more than half used words like these to describe how they feel ...

regret
dirty
used
guilty
empty
ashamed
alone
miserable
duped
And even ... abused.

Some have to take a bath to feel clean, and some struggle for a sense of forgiveness for months. In fact, Donna Freitas found most had dashed hopes after casual sexual encounters. One young man writes, "I often feel as though I've betrayed myself and my values by being physically intimate with someone I do not share an emotional intimacy with."[43] One young woman, in her journal, writes: "[I] feel bad about myself (like a sleaze) ... Feel empty ... I degraded myself."[44]

There is not a chance under the kingdom's sun that Jesus wants anyone to feel degraded because of a sexual relationship. There's something seriously wrong with sex when the gift of God makes us feel ashamed or dirty. Sex is designed for pleasure and the intimacy of love, and scientific research is just beginning to unravel some of sex's mysteries.

SEX AND SCIENCE

Some in medical research examine what goes on when two people engage in sexual behaviors. First, from simple and casual skin-to-skin touching to the heightened pleasures of orgasm, the brain releases a neurochemical called dopamine, which tells your brain that what you are doing feels very good. To grasp the magnitude of the body's chemical response, we need to know that sexual pleasure and drugs both generate the same dopamine experience. The pleasure of sex, therefore, is like the pleasure of an addicting drug. At its simplest, dopamine is designed by God to create the desire to have more sex. But there's more to sex neurochemically than pleasure.

The brains of both men and women release neurochemicals during sexual behaviors that also say: "I am bonding emotionally with you." Oxytocin tells a woman's brain that the man is hers and vasopressin tells the man's brain that the woman is his.

Here is an alarming medical conclusion: Bonding occurs chemically *whenever* sexual relations occur — not just when a person chooses bonding to occur and not just when a person is intimately in love with another person.

One more brain item: When anyone engages in sexual behaviors, the brain creates pathways of connection that render that experience easier to repeat and, in fact, that render that experience something the brain wants to repeat over and over. That is, synaptic pathways, or tunnels of sexual pleasure, are created in the brain simply by engaging in sexual behaviors.

Which leads to a problem. When a young man or a young woman begins to sleep around or share sexual experiences with more than one person, shame and feeling dirty result because our God-designed brain gets confused. That sense of feeling dirty is partly the neurochemicals in the brain saying, "I'm confused. Who is this new person you are having sex with?"

What we all need to keep in mind is that our brain and neurochemicals remember the synaptic pathways of former lovers. This is exactly what the comments of the young adults above were leading to. Those who engage in sexual behaviors are opening brain flow that can become massively complex and frustrating for the person who wants to create multiple bonding experiences. The question the young people I quoted above are asking is the right one: Does this behavior create obstacles for future healthy intimacy and obstacles for the possibility of long-term faithful, loving relationship?

The answer, according to science, is *yes*. Sex devoid of relational commitment confuses our brain's neurochemicals and begins to corrode our capacity for one of our deepest yearnings: the yearning for commitment and faithfulness, or bonding with someone who loves us. Let me put this more forcefully:

It is impossible to engage in the hookup culture
without damaging your brain's innate desire
for healthy, faithful, emotional bonding.

Alicia makes this confession: "I also realized that hooking up had influenced my notions of self-worth, love, relationships and expectations of men in ways I hadn't realized."[45]

I assure you, there's a better way. It's the kingdom way.

SEX AND LOVE

Jesus's view of sex and love were profoundly Jewish, and that means they emerged out of Israel's story and Israel's Scriptures, what Christians today call the Old Testament. In that context, love and sex were about consummating marriage, procreation, expression of love and pleasure — but all of this in the context of a rugged, realistic lifetime commitment where the body really does matter.[46]

Let's begin with the idea that the body really does matter, because for some Christians the body is inferior to the soul or spirit or mind. Therefore, to them, what the body does doesn't really matter. That's a form of Gnosticism.

For others, while they think what they do with their body does matter, they can't integrate their spirituality into their embodiedness. So, instead of seeing their body as important to following Jesus, they let it tag along to the spirituality game they play but hope the body keeps quiet the whole time and perhaps sits in the corner without attracting attention to itself.

The one thing Jesus learned in the Jewish world was that the body isn't a container for the spirit but that the body is fully integrated with spirit. For Jesus, there is complete integration of body and spirit. So, it can be put this way: The reason Jesus and his Jewish world talked about sex and bodies so much was because the body was so important. Your body matters and what you do with your body is your spirituality!

Jesus' view of rugged, realistic commitment can be found in what he taught about divorce. At the time of Jesus there were two basic views, as there are in most cultures on most issues most of the time. One group believed that divorce should be granted permissively and for any good reason, and that a permissible divorce meant a permissible remarriage. A famous rabbi, Hillel, is credited with this view. Another group, led by a rabbi named Shammai, thought the only permissible ground of divorce (and remarriage) was what Moses taught in Deuteronomy 24:1. The verse indicates that a man might become displeased with his wife if he "finds *something indecent*" about her. On those two Hebrew words, *erwat dabar* ("something indecent"), the fate of families hung. For Shammai, something indecent meant sexual immorality like adultery or incest. But for Hillel it meant whatever displeased the man — and the expansiveness of that was later illustrated to be as broad as: "Even if she burns your toast!"

In this context of a raging debate about permissiveness in divorce and remarriage, we get this report from Matthew 19:

"Some Pharisees came to him to test him. They asked, 'Is it lawful for a man to divorce his wife for any and every reason?'" (v. 3).

That is, they are asking if Hillel is right: Can you get a permissible divorce for most any reason you can find? Jesus' response astounded even his disciples, and he gives his answer in three parts, and these three all illustrate that Jesus believed that marriage was permanent and that sexual relations and love make sense only within that context:

#1: God makes the marriage.

"Therefore what God has joined together, let no one separate" (v. 6).

#2: Divorce was only permitted due to sin.

"Moses permitted you to divorce your wives because your hearts were hard. But it was not this way from the beginning" (v. 8).

#3: Marriage is permanent.

"I tell you that anyone who divorces his wife, except for sexual immorality, and marries another woman commits adultery" (v. 9).

His disciples, because they had imbibed the permissiveness of their own culture, were shocked. They said:

"If this is the situation between a husband and wife, it is better not to marry" (v. 10).

So Jesus took their comment to the opposite, morally zealous extreme:

Not everyone can accept this word, but only those to whom it has
been given. For some are eunuchs because they were born that way;
others have been made eunuchs; and others have renounced marriage because of the kingdom of heaven. The one who can accept
this should accept it.

(vv. 11 – 12)

If those words don't illustrate the moral zeal of Jesus and his
belief that marriage is for keeps, then nothing does.

But this forces another issue to arise. "Okay," you might say, "I
can see that Jesus' moral zeal led him to believe marriage was permanent and that sex only made sense within a context of rugged
commitment to one another forever. I can see that. But where's the
love? It's got to be more than just keeping the law."

You're right, and this is why we not only have to listen to Jesus in
light of his historical context but also in light of his Bible.

The biggest problem with understanding sex today is that we
don't understand what love is. Here's where we are headed: Love is
not what we call romance, neither is it dopamine highs. Brain sci-
entists will tell us right up front that both of those expressions are
mostly chemical.

What then is love? Love is a rugged commitment to be with
someone. "Being with" is what love is all about. And in a Christian
context for someone who follows Jesus, love is being with someone
as we both follow Jesus. The Bible sketches a wonderful view of love,
and it's one we need to listen to more carefully.

Israel's story had one book that was devoted to this theme of
rugged, committed love and marriage and sex, and it is a book that
presents what can only be called a kingdom ideal of love, sex, and
relationship: the Song of Solomon. This book, which is a series of
beautiful, evocative, and erotic poems, shaped Jews to see that love
and sex belonged together. This was in dramatic contrast to what
they were finding in Greece and Rome at the time. The Song of Solomon reveals two humans—a man and his wife—who are obsessed
with one another in rapturous love, who playfully delight in one
another's presence and bodies, and whose words are so other-oriented

and vulnerable that one must describe this book as Songs of Delight and Songs about Loving You.

It doesn't take much imagination to know what these two love-birds are saying to one another as they coo love poems to one another from Song of Solomon (Song of Songs) 4:16–5:1.

She
> Awake, north wind,
> and come, south wind!
> Blow on my garden,
> that its fragrance may spread abroad.
> Let my beloved come into his garden
> and taste its choice fruits.

He
> I have come into my garden, my sister, my bride;
> I have gathered my myrrh with my spice.
> I have eaten my honeycomb and my honey;
> I have drunk my wine and my milk.

Friends
> Eat, friends, and drink;
> drink your fill of love.

Or this from Song of Solomon 7:6–9, 10–12:

He
> How beautiful you are and how pleasing,
> my love, with your delights!
> Your stature is like that of the palm,
> and your breasts like clusters of fruit.
> I said, "I will climb the palm tree;
> I will take hold of its fruit."
> May your breasts be like clusters of grapes on the vine,
> the fragrance of your breath like apples,
> and your mouth like the best wine.

She
> May the wine go straight to my beloved,
> flowing gently over lips and teeth.
> I belong to my beloved,
> and his desire is for me.
> Come, my beloved, let us go to the countryside,

let us spend the night in the villages.
Let us go early to the vineyards
to see if the vines have budded,
if their blossoms have opened,
and if the pomegranates are in bloom—
there I will give you my love.

In one of my college classes, after I read the last two chapters of the Song of Solomon in a dramatic fashion, one young man at the back of the room, with dopamine now at work in his system, uttered: "Man, am I glad this is in the Bible!"

The good news is that it is. The good news also is that it is designed to guide the sexual behaviors of humans. The Song of Solomon is ancient Israel's "love and sex" manual. But there is one thing that shapes the dopamine delights of this most sacred of sex manuals: a committed relationship that expressed itself in being "with" one another. These two poets come alive in loving one another. In other words, the themes are shaped by chemically induced commitments that are found in the release of vasopressin and oxytocin: "I am my beloved's and my beloved is mine."

Sex is about relationship.
Sex is about love.
Without relationship and love, sex wounds.

Student after student tells me the same story, sometimes without even using words.

THE THREE HARDEST WORDS TO SAY TODAY: "I.LOVE.YOU."

Humans, Jesus' dream constantly affirms, are made to love one another, and only in loving others do humans become fully human. Humans are wired to connect with one another and in that relational connection the electricity of love flows and lights up the human being. (Sex is only one part of this electric connection.) But somehow four lies about love have been hoisted from the depths of nonsense and downloaded into the culture of our world. They are these:

I love you means ...
Lie #1: I am needy.
Lie #2: I am weak.
Lie #3: I am dependent (or codependent).
Lie #4: I lose my independence.

Our culture has rammed this list of system-crashing lies into the minds and hearts of this generation. Yes, some humans connect to others out of an unhealthy neediness or weakness and become codependent and lose their sense of self. But, God made us to love others and to connect to others and it is not wrong to be social and to fall in love so much that you feel like you can't exist without another person—I know I felt that way when I fell in love with my wife, Kris. I just didn't want to live without her (and still don't). I was fifteen and Kris was fifteen; we were sophomores in high school. I couldn't wait to see her between classes and after school and on the weekends. The world, so it seemed to me, wasn't complete unless Kris was in it.

We've been with one another for more than three decades, which means we've done lots of things together. Every evening for the last eight years, usually around 4:00 p.m., I make our dinner salad. I get out the spinach leaves and the cutting board and the knife and the bowl, and I wash the leaves and then cut the leaves carefully into smaller bits. Then I get out broccoli slaw and tomatoes and onions and Pecorino Romano cheese and dried berries and nuts and broccoli florets and carrots. Then I begin to chop away, and in about fifteen minutes the salad is ready.

You might be wondering why I've only been doing this for eight years, so I'll tell you: Kris and I had been married for twenty-eight years before it dawned on me to help in the kitchen. Kris is a psychologist, and she knew just how to handle my eagerness at that point. She encouraged me, and within two days the job was mine! What I'm telling you is that love is not simply about dopamine rushes and about special moments of intimacy. Love in the Bible is about being *with* someone in a lifetime commitment, and the routine activities of our days—like making salad—are inherent to what it means to be *with* someone. I am with Kris in these sorts of ways, and it is this kind of "withness" that shapes our marriage and our love.

Many today think we have progressed beyond those days of rapturously loving another person so much we don't feel complete without them or committing ourselves to be with another person for a lifetime. Leonora Epstein, in a CNN.com column,[47] was speaking with her therapist about her struggles in relationships and thinking the feminist therapist might just delve into some "childhood father complex" when her therapist uttered these jaw-dropping words: "Some women are just happier in a relationship."

Epstein questioned herself: "Huh? Isn't the modern woman supposed to be totally amazing on her own?" Then she thought through her own story to discover this: "When in committed relationships, I was happier. When single, I was depressed." What was most jaw-dropping in her reflections was this conclusion: "And perhaps 'needing a man' is an indication of the more basic human instinct — not for reproduction, but for companionship." Leonora is not about to give up on her "better alone" thinking though: "The idea still doesn't sit right with me as someone who has put so much energy into making me happy."

The message of our culture is to do it on your own and to get your affirmations from yourself and your accomplishments: "Don't make the commitment for life but just see how long it lasts." So we have a generation of highly inspired workaholics who are struggling with the decision to avoid companionship as a central goal of life and, as other studies are showing, they are becoming more and more depressed because of the absence of committed relationships.

Instead of being taught that the aim of life is to love God and to love others, including (if chosen) a bonding relationship with one person as a commitment to be "with" that person for life, our culture teaches that committed love is a constraint on a life already full with all kinds of goals. Instead of being taught that sex flows from genuine love and that genuine love craves commitment, our culture hears that raspy voice of Tina Turner: "What's love got to do with it?"

For instance, a woman named Sienna said it this way: "Commitment to a boyfriend, carried out with the same intensity, seemed like one expectation too much."[48] That is to say, some believe they can't afford to invest time, energy, and emotion in a deep relationship. "Hooking up appears to be a practical alternative."[49]

A young man named Tom, who likes sex, puts it flippantly because his focus is on other things: "I think that guys don't want to worry about having a girlfriend so much. It's, like, somewhat of a burden."[50] The burden or constraint of committed love, which alone satisfies human relationships, has become an optional part of life for many. Laura Sessions Stepp says this so well: "Sigmund Freud is said to have believed that a happy life is made up of two things: love and work. Society has asked [today's] young women to choose between the two, and they've chosen work, at least for the short term."[51] The instinct to work is clashing with the potentially soul-satisfying demands of lasting love.

Our culture, and clearly this can be exaggerated, finds "I love you" to be the hardest three words to say. Why? This generation knows what real love costs and that it means committing to be with someone forever. A young Duke University woman named Anne Katharine Wales says this: "Somewhere along the line most of us have gotten really close to someone, maybe even fallen in love. . . . For some reason, this scares us beyond belief. Somehow this doesn't fit with our plan of achieving our dreams. We want to be independent; we want to go off and change the world in our own way. But we never planned on falling for someone else."[52] The result is a generation that is wary and cynical and selfish and anxious about love. That wariness is wounding this generation deeply and hooking up is not satisfying its yearnings.

ROMANCE, ANYONE?

Studies show that the deepest kind of romance desired today is that a young woman wants a boyfriend and a young man wants a girlfriend, and they want to hold hands in public, going on official dates, and just plain talking with one another. In other words, they want someone who will be "with" them in a loyal way.

Donna Freitas interviewed a sexy young woman named Amy. She's hot and she likes to dress the part and young men like her to be hot and dress the part. She knows it. It "helps me feel good about myself," she says. "I just want to be fun." Freitas observes that "being fun" has led Amy down a painful path, and she offers a potent observation that lies at the core of Amy's dream: "There is one major thing that the girl who seems to have everything is missing: a boyfriend." After getting to know Amy, Freitas says: "Amy really wants to find a boyfriend, someone who will love her. She's tried everything she knows: hooking up, being friends with benefits, playing hard to get. Nothing has worked." She continues: "[Amy wanted] a real boyfriend, one who loved her and respected her, and who would admit to their relationship in public by doing something as simple as asking her on a date or holding her hand while walking across campus."[53] What Amy wants is the norm, but our culture — your culture — works against it.

Donna Freitas discovered in talking to college students that the number one romantic experience was "just talking" and "talking for hours." In fact, Hephzibah Anderson, in her confession of a year-long commitment to chastity, described how relationships without sex were more romantic and emotionally satisfying, because, as she puts it: "When you've closed yourself off physically, it's easier to open up emotionally."[54]

This is where a good dose of Jesus' kingdom vision deconstructs a culture gone terribly awry. For Jesus, the kingdom vision of love, justice, peace, and wisdom shapes everything. Personal relationships, because they emerge out of that vision, will also be shaped by love, justice, peace, and wisdom. Romance is a desire and love is a desire because God wired us to connect with others, and to connect deeply — emotionally, spiritually, physically, and sexually. But emotional, spiritual, physical, and sexual love only work well between two who are committed enough to start a family and to be with one another forever. (I'm not suggesting that singleness is wrong; I am saying that lovelessness, in the sense of lasting commitment, is contrary to how we are designed.)

When I was blogging about how love and sex have become disconnected and how love in our culture has become something to fear rather than something to pursue, a professor at a Midwest liberal arts university, Anette Ejsing, offered a set of stunning observations about what is going on with young women today in a world where sexual relations have hopped the rails of decency. She writes that what is being described in the hook-up culture "is a state of being no woman can sustain." With wisdom, Anette warns of the breakdown of love that will happen to those in the hook-up culture. She says:

> It must [or, will] morph into something else, which could include the following:
>
> - Men cannot be trusted, I want to stick closer to my girlfriends than my male partners. Maybe I even want to explore sexual relationships with women I can trust because they also feel the same way.
> - People cannot be trusted, so I would rather be an island unto others.
> - I feel unworthy of someone's love, so I will not dare to hope in love (from a partner, or others).
> - Depression! (It only takes a brief glance at stats on the use of anti-depressants among young adults and college students to realize this is happening a lot.)
>
> Sexuality is a much more integral part of who we are as human beings than we generally care to admit.

What would Jesus say? Jesus is weeping. Why? Not simply because purity codes have been crossed but because what lies behind the traditional Jewish (biblical) laws about sex express what matters most to Jesus: love, justice, peace, and wisdom. Our culture has distorted love from the inside out.

There's a better way.

THE KINGDOM CHOICE: CHASING ROMANCE OR SETTLING INTO FIDELITY?

We observed above that emerging adults today want romance, but I'd like to suggest that the word *romance* is not the right word because it doesn't go far enough. What emerging adults want, so it seems to me, is the fidelity inherent in a loving, faithful, intimate relationship. What they want is someone to be *with* for a lifetime. In fact, our culture confuses romance with love. Which leads me to one more fundamental idea about love and marriage and sex. Along about the medieval age love morphed its way into the Platonic, courtly romantic ideal where love became intoxication with the intoxicating feelings of loving another person.[55]

Some married men and married women then had two kinds of relationships: one with a husband or wife and one with a lover (with whom they might never physically consummate their relationship). Instead, they tantalized and titillated themselves with the emotional surges connected to falling in love. Often they would put obstacles in their own paths in order to intensify their feelings, equating those romantic feelings with love itself. What mattered was the burning fire of feelings instead of the joy of the beloved.

This romantic theory of love, which finds its way into Hollywood and novels, distorts the rugged choice of settling into fidelity. This romantic theory of love puts emotions and feelings and (my) personal happiness at the center of what love is. In other words, romantic love more often than not *uses* another person to fulfill one's own desires and passions.

Jesus' world is against this romantic theory of relationships. What flows directly from Jesus' kingdom dream is a rugged and settled commitment to the other person rather than to my own swarming feelings and to my own happiness. Instead of loving love, as in courtly love, the kingdom lover loves the other and lives his or her life for that other—the way the lovers in the Song of Solomon take delight in the other. (Notice how often in the poetry from Song of Solomon the lovers speak of the other.)

Instead of loving the absence of the other, as is the case with romantic love, because it generates emotional yearning for the other, kingdom lovers delight in the daily, routine presence of one another, whether the emotions of romance are present or not. Eating together, walking together, sitting together, praying together, sleeping together, and living a life together is the way we settle into fidelity. There is only one guarantee for sustaining marriage in a kingdom way: the promise to stay married trumping emotional happiness. Why? Because the lover believes the other's good is the chief concern. One of the world's experts on the societal history of love is the French scholar Denis de Rougemont, who makes this profound observation from the perspective of a man (whom a woman loves in return): "To choose a woman for a wife is to say to Miss So-and-So: 'I want to live with you just as you are.' For this really means: 'It is you I choose *to share* my life with me, and that [sharing of life] is the only *evidence* there can be that I love you.'"[56]

As I write this paragraph, Kris and I have been married for thirty-six years. Recently my class was talking about wedding vows, and the subject of whether or not to use standard vows or to write your own vows came up. Which led us to read a traditional vow:

To have and to behold,
from this day on,
for better or for worse,
for richer, for poorer,
in sickness and in health,
to love and to cherish;
until death do us part.

As we were reading the vow and the students were discussing with one another what their views were, this came to my mind: Yes, that's our story, that's our vow, that's what Kris and I have lived. Ups and downs, good days and bad days, months when we hoped we'd have enough money and months when we relaxed. As I pondered these words and students were talking about whether they'd use traditional vows or write their own, I thought about what marriage was. In my view, only one expression can sum up the real story of marriage:

I will be with you.

Underneath the dopamine and beyond the neurochemicals is the commitment I made to Kris and that she made to me, and it is the commitment that has sustained us: it is the commitment to be with one another until the end. We now have a story to tell of our One. Life *with* one another.

The great Danish philosopher Soren Kierkegaard never married, but while engaged he contemplated marriage in ways that few can surpass: "What I am through her she is through me, and neither of us is anything by oneself, but we are what we are in union."[57] Kierkegaard unlocks one of the doors to love: If we are humans through other humans, we are lovers through loving the one we love and through receiving the love of the one who loves us. "I.love.you" will become our words when the *you* is what the *I* most cares about.

I contend that the kingdom dream of Jesus reshapes what love is, what intimacy is, what marriage is, and what sex is, because Jesus' vision of the kingdom transforms the meaning of love.

Interlude

Jesus is a healer and every page of the Gospels shows that. Behind Jesus' gift of healing people is grace. Jesus heals by touching people with God's healing grace.

When you add up this kingdom dream of Jesus—justice, peace, love, and wisdom—and then add to that kingdom dream the summons of Jesus to live sexually wholesome lives and to shape our vocations by that kingdom dream, you may well encounter your mistakes, your sins, your stupidities, your foolishnesses, your acts of injustice, and your decisions to wage war instead of pursuing peace. Like some of the young men and women in the previous chapter, you may feel ashamed or you may feel dirty about some things you have done or the kind of person you have been.

This is where Jesus the healer comes in. Jesus' closest follower, Peter, preached the first sermon ever to Gentiles, and he told them that Jesus was a healer. He reminded them how ...

"God anointed Jesus of Nazareth with the Holy Spirit and power, and how he went around doing good and healing all who were under the power of the devil, because God was with him" (Acts 10:38).

Then Peter told them ...

"Everyone who believes in [Jesus] receives forgiveness of sins through his name"(Acts 10:43).

Whether you've got lots of baggage from sexual behaviors or whether you are now discovering that have searched for happiness through making lots of money ...

Whether you're chasing a career that won't satisfy what God has made you to do or you have acted in ways that are unloving, unjust, unpeaceful, and unwise ...

Jesus is the healer and he offers you forgiveness
because his death on the cross can forgive us of our sins.

My favorite way of saying this is that Jesus became what we are so we could become what he is—he became what we are to make us what we should be. He entered into our human condition, he entered into our struggles and he entered into our joys, and on the cross he entered into the death we deserved for our sins. His act of identifying with us is the primal word of grace. Accept that grace by turning to Jesus as the healer, as the grace-giver, and as the one who forgives. And there's more: Jesus not only forgives. Jesus broke the power of sin and death by rising from the dead so he can empower us to live out the kingdom dream.

One of my favorite figures around Jesus is John the Baptist. John's idea was to get everyone to go back to the Jordan River experience where Israel first entered into the land. What John was telling people was that they needed to turn from their injustices and unloving behaviors, to ask God to wash them from their sins by entering into the baptismal waters of the river Jordan, and to start all over again. That's exactly what Jesus the grace-healer does for us: he gives us the permission to start all over again. When we come to him, he forgives us and says, "Let's start all over again. This time, though, give your One.Life to the Kingdom.Life."

This is why the earliest followers of Jesus got baptized. They entered into Jesus' death for them and they entered into Jesus' resurrection in their baptism. This is also why they were so taken by Jesus' last supper. They were invited to eat some bread and to drink some wine. By doing that, they "ingested and imbibed" his death and his resurrection as the primal acts of God's grace and God's healing. Jesus the healer invites us into the water to be washed, and he invites us to the table to eat and to drink to find forgiveness and sustenance. Those actions heal us so we can live Jesus' kingdom dream.

CHAPTER 11

VOCATION.LIFE

I had just put down the phone after a conversation with a former student. She was finishing a law degree at a prestigious school. She had done an internship (or whatever it is called for lawyers) but was discouraged. Though she was nearing the end of her J.D. (Juris Doctorate), she was hesitating about completing her degree. She said she now wanted to move on to "do something that really *matters*."

I kept thinking that a law degree permits a person to interpret and apply law to our culture, the nobility of which often eludes even budding lawyers. Isn't that something that really matters? I asked her what her parents were thinking.

"They want me to do whatever makes me happy."

She didn't think their advice was practical. I told her what I thought of her talents and character, which are both outstanding, and then I advised her to finish her J.D. and be a lawyer for two years, pay off all her school debts, and then reevaluate. I told her that a vocation wrapped up in our legal system could be a noble life.

Throughout that afternoon, though, I kept thinking about what it means to do something that matters. I wondered about my paternal grandpa who was a coal miner and my grandma who didn't get past the fourth grade. My grandparents nurtured a bundle of kids and made ends meet. I think what they did matters.

I know people who are lawyers and who drive big machines and who are school teachers and who are coaches and who are selling insurance and who are accountants and who are science research professors and who are dentists and who are pastors and who are missionaries. What each of these people does matters. I kept thinking about this word *matters*. I'm unconvinced that some jobs—the so-called "spiritual" ones—are valuable while others are "secular" and therefore not as valuable. I recently read the memoir of James Brown—known to football fans as J. B. and the host of CBS Sports' *The NFL Today*—and I kept thinking that what he does also "matters." When James Brown was dancing between a secure life in the business world and the more unpredictable life of reporting on TV, he realized that "there comes a point when you have to embrace risk and your dreams."[58] He chose his dream, cut himself away from his business career, and it has made all the difference.

This topic of vocation (or job or career) comes up often in my office, with students and in the hallways, with other professors, and we are all convinced that the current generation has some special ideas about jobs.

First, they want to make lots of money because it's the only life they've ever known—that is, if they've grown up middle class. Second, they want a career that combines what is fun with what is challenging. Third, they want to do things that "matter" or are significant for the world. My university captures this yearning in our motto: "Lives of Significance and Service." And, fourth, we professors have observed that our students want to grow in their careers and find more and more joy as their careers progress.

Many my age (or younger or older) may be tempted to slap a leg, raise an eyebrow, and utter: "Good luck!" But deep inside we love the hopefulness of young adults. I believe there is a way of making everything you do matter, and it comes by attending once again to the kingdom dream of Jesus. But recent conclusions reveal that many are struggling to discover a career that matters. Perhaps the search for the elusive dream-career that matters is, well, unexamined, and perhaps this unexamined career is what is causing all the confusion in the above conclusions. So I want to make a claim for you to consider:

The unexamined vocation leads to what does not "matter."

BUT

The examined vocation will "matter."

Perhaps the reason so many today flounder from one job to another is because instead of examining what they do in light of the kingdom, they fail to realize that what they are doing really does matter. (Unless they are paid to be professional spammers, which can't be kingdom work.) It is time to reconsider what we do in light of the kingdom dream of Jesus, and I believe his kingdom vision can turn what we do into something that matters and can give our One. Life purpose.

SEE YOUR VOCATION THROUGH THE KINGDOM DREAM

Remember your dreams are glimpses of the Jesus kingdom dream. Your vocation, which in so many ways is unique to you, can genuinely matter if you keep your eyes on the kingdom of God as your guiding North Star. Teaching matters when you treat your students as humans whom you love and whom you are helping. Coaching soccer matters when you connect kids to the kingdom. Growing vegetables becomes kingdom work when we enjoy God's green world as a gift from him. Collecting taxes becomes kingdom work when you treat each person as someone who is made in the image (the *Eikon* in Greek) of God and as a citizen instead of as a suspect. Jobs become vocations and begin to matter when we connect what we do to God's kingdom vision for this world. Sure, there's scut work involved—like learning English grammar well enough to write clean sentences and reading great writers who can show you how good prose works. Like hours in the weight room and running sprints so you can become good enough to compete at high levels and learn the game of soccer so you can pass it on. Like long hours in the office in your early career to learn the ropes and master the job. Like hours with small children when we are challenged to make some mind-numbing routines into habits of the heart and kingdom.

It is easy to see missional work in the slums of India as something that matters. Perhaps the desire to do something that matters is why so many of us get involved in missional work like that. But most of us don't have a vocation like that, and that means most of us do lots of scut work as a matter of routine. We have to believe that the mundane matters to God, and the way to make the mundane matter is to baptize what we do in the kingdom vision of Jesus. Kathleen Norris, whose writings breathe fresh—realistic—sparkles of life over many, put this well: "We want life to have meaning, want fulfillment, healing and even ecstasy, but the human paradox is that we find these things by starting where we are, not where we wish to be."[59]

Some students, if I'm honest, bore me. I wonder why they are in my classes and I wonder if I'm wasting my time. I began my teaching career in a seminary, and a standard course I taught was called Greek Exegesis. Which meant we opened up the Greek New Testament and read it, and I interrogated students on how the grammar worked.

I loved it, and one of my students, Mark, didn't. He liked the Chicago Cubs stories I told, but he didn't like Greek. And he told me that—and I didn't like it because I was doing what I dreamed when I got to teach Greek. He was a good student so he got by, and I tossed him into the pantry of former students. Then one day I saw him in town, and we chatted. He was pastoring and seemed to be doing well, in spite of never having thought Greek was important. Then a few years later he called me about a church he had started, and it was going well. He asked me to speak at his church over the next three years, and each time I spoke at his church the church was growing. No, I would have to say it was flourishing.

One day he asked to play golf, and during the round he said something that made teaching Mark worthwhile: "I remember when you said, way back in seminary class ..." and I barely heard what he said next. This is why: When he was a student, I thought he was bored and wasn't even listening. Yet, he was. And it helped him and it was still helping him. Even when we think we are wasting someone's time, our scut work is to do what we are called to do and let God water and sun what we do. And God does.

Because God is at work in whatever we do, we need to see we are doing much more than making money.

IT'S NOT ABOUT MONEY (COMPLETELY)

Only 15 percent of American *households* have a six-figure income and only about 5 percent of American *individuals* have a six-figure income.

Instead of focusing our lives on a six-figure dream, followers of Jesus need to focus on the Kingdom.Life, which turns the six-figure dream inside out. Jesus' dream involved a radical detachment from possessions:

> But seek first his kingdom
> and his righteousness,
> and all these things [clothing, food, shelter]
> will be given to you as well.
>
> *Matthew 6:33*

It involved a willingness to contribute to the needs of others and virtually to renounce a life soaked in making money:

> Sell your possessions and give to the poor.
>
> *Luke 12:33*

While many in the history of the Church have given up everything they owned in order to serve others, and I think of St. Basil the Great and St. Francis of Assisi, the rest of us are challenged to cut back and to tone it down so we can take from our abundance and provide for those who are in need.

When the Lord of the Christian is a poor man, the wealth of his followers is brought into embarrassing clarity. When the kingdom dream of Jesus shapes our vocations, it turns us from folks who strive for wealth into folks whose vocations are used for others.

PEOPLE ARE NEIGHBORS

At the very core of your One.Life and the kingdom dream are human beings and our personal relationships with others. Relationship talk isn't sappy TV talk; relationships go to the guts of eternity, where we discover that the Three-in-One-God is Life.

There are very few ideas that move me so deeply they create silence, and this may be because I think I've landed on one of the deep secrets of life. The one silencing idea is the Trinity, the Christian belief that God is One and Three, Three and One, at the same time, always and forever. My soul goes silent when I meander in thought to pre-creation, when all that existed was this Three-in-One God, and I ask this question: Before it all began, before the stars and sun and sky and earth, before what Genesis 1 calls the *tohu vabohu*, or the "formless void," *what was God doing all alone?*

Theologians have studied this and have landed upon one word that best approximates what God was doing. That word is *perichoresis*. That word describes the interpenetrating and mutual indwelling of the Father, the Son, and the Spirit in One Another.

So what was God doing? God was *perichoreting*.

The Father and the Son and the Spirit were in an endless dance of endless love and surging joy and delightful play as they enjoyed the depth of their love for One Another. They were doing this forever and are doing this now and will do this eternally. At the core of life, in God's own life, is this throbbing joy of mutual indwelling.

When I finish meandering, and I find myself doing this at least once a week, I land on this: Love is God's gift to you and to me to enjoy the *perichoreting* of God. We get to do what God does when we love, because when we love we participate in mutual indwelling and interpenetrating one another. When we love, we enter into the Dance of Eternity. No wonder, I say to myself, sex symbolizes the relationship of the persons in the Trinity and no wonder sex symbolizes the relationship of God to the people of God. Sex is one of our high moments of interpenetration.

When Rob Bell and John Piper, two famous pastors today, speak of sex as either "this is that," meaning sexuality points us toward spirituality (Bell) or "the mystery of Christ and the Church" (Piper), they are tapping into the deepest mystery of life by connecting what we get to do—marriage and sex and love—to *who God is.*[60]

This deep mystery of life reveals that Life itself is personal. The deepest dimension of the kingdom dream and of life itself is that we are persons who dwell with other persons, and only in loving others do we tap into the core of that mystery. When we do, we know it.

If you want your job to "matter," then keep in mind that life itself is about *perichoreting* with others—with your spouse or with your family or with your friends or with your community of faith or with your city or with your country or with the world *and with those with whom you work*. What we do matters when what we do is seen as something designed for persons.

AN EXAMPLE: HARRIET BEECHER STOW

President Millard Fillmore, the thirteenth president of the ⌐ States (1850–1853), signed the Fugitive Slave Act into law in September 1850. Section five of that law commanded citizens "to aid and assist in the prompt and efficient execution of this law, whenever their services may be required." To translate: If you find an escaped slave, it's your duty to return the slave to his or her master. The Fugitive Slave Act got under the skin of those who opposed slavery in a way that precipitated the end of slavery and the beginning of the Civil War, and no one was more irritated about this Fugitive Slave Act than Harriet Beecher Stowe.[61]

So what did she do? Harriet did what she was gifted to do and, because of the dominant male power, she did what a woman could do. When the Fugitive Slave Act became law in Boston, Harriet's sister Isabella Beecher Hooker wrote a letter to Harriet that was read to the family one evening: "Now, Hattie, if I could use a pen as you can, I would write something that would make this whole nation feel what an accursed thing slavery is."

Stowe's biographer continues: "One of the Stowe children remembered that when this letter was read aloud in the parlor, Harriet 'rose up from her chair' and declared 'I will write something. I will if I live.'" Live she did and write she did. Her book was called *Uncle Tom's Cabin,* and it brought into perfect display the art of storytelling Harriet Beecher Stowe had mastered over the previous years in publishing stories. She had a knack at recording how ordinary people talked and she used her stories to shoot arrows at the heart. She began writing her famous novel by sending in weekly installments to the *National Era*, and her goal was to "show the *best side* of the thing and something *faintly approaching the worst*."

The result was nothing less than stupendous—some 500,000 women in England, Ireland, and Scotland joined her crusade to battle slavery. She was the right person at the right time, and she chose the right method for the greatest number of people. She simply told stories that turned the white slave owner into performing inexcusable behaviors and the slave condition into a heart-rending life. According to her biographer, John Hedrick, through this novel Stowe became "the single most powerful voice on behalf of the slave," and, unlike so many, she had the courage to act on her convictions. She gave her One.Life to the vocation she was gifted to live.

Stowe went straight to the White House to Abraham Lincoln. Lincoln, in a set of lines I was not taught as a schoolboy growing up in his state of Illinois, declared his own allegiance in these words:

> *My paramount object in this struggle is to save the Union, and it is not either to save or destroy slavery. If I could save the Union without freeing any slave, I would do it; ... What I do about slavery and the colored race, I do because I believe it helps to save the Union; and what I forbear I forbear because I do not believe it would help to save the Union.*

Stowe's allegiance was higher, however, and she wasn't satisfied. She challenged Lincoln by publishing a response that turned his words inside out, and they became some of the more memorable words in that historical struggle:

> *My paramount object in this struggle is to set at liberty them that are bruised, and not either to save or destroy the Union. What I do in favor of the Union, I do because it helps to free the oppressed; what I forbear, I forbear because it does not help to free the oppressed. I shall do less for the Union whenever it would hurt the cause of the slave, and more when I believe it would help the cause of the slave.*

Let no one doubt the power of the pen or the vocation of the novelist. Stowe's words, alongside a personal visit with the President and Mrs. Lincoln in the White House just a month before the Emancipation Proclamation's official announcement, surely had an impact on Lincoln.

Harriet Beecher Stowe, propelled by Christian convictions, relentless courage, and dogged determination to do something that mattered, did what she could do — her gifts were swallowed up by the kingdom vision of Jesus. She didn't care about money and she knew the African (American) was her neighbor. That vision, dipped in ink, made her a force. As I teach my classes, I sometimes ponder who might be the next Harriet Beecher Stowe. Or the next Alan Paton, whose *Cry, the Beloved Country*, the story of apartheid's impact in South Africa, began to shatter the powers of racism. Or the next Harper Lee, author of *To Kill a Mockingbird*. I wonder who might be the one who will speak to our world and our culture and our country about the evils and injustices that need to be eradicated. Perhaps it will be you.

DO WHAT YOU DO WELL

I grew up with the idea that I could only be happy if I found "God's will." People do weird things because they think they are doing God's will. I once met a man who told me God spoke to him about starting a fishing business in the Caribbean, and it so happened that he was from Minnesota, didn't like the cold, and loved fishing. And it sure seemed to me that he blamed God for what he was doing, when perhaps he was calling the shots himself. (And from the look in his wife's eyes, she agreed with me.) Still, leaving aside such examples, there's something to focusing our attentive heart on God so that we can learn of God and listen to God and discern what God created us to do in this world.

This may be the most important thing we can learn about God's will:

> God's will . . .
> and what you dream about in your deepest dreams
> line up so well,
> you can usually chase your dreams
> and you will more often than not
> find God's will.

There is a reason why so many people quote Frederick Buechner's famous line about God's will, because it tells a deep truth. Buechner said God's will is this: "The place where God calls you is where your deep gladness meets the world's deep hunger."[62] This beautifully combines the kingdom dream of Jesus and your own personal dream—find that place and do that. Another wise thinker about finding a life that matters is Parker Palmer, who borrowed an old Quaker idea when he said that we find a life that matters when "we let our life speak."[63]

If you keep your eye on the kingdom of God, if you keep in mind that deeply personal nature of all you do, then you can pursue that place where your deepest gladness and the world's deepest needs meet, and in that place your life will speak. You are asked merely to discern the intersection of what God is doing—kingdom of God— and what you are asked to do in what God's doing.

DO THAT

There are too many places where we find the world's deepest hunger, and many of them appeal to us as the place where we might find our deepest gladness. When we try to do too many good things, we burn out or we tune out or we leave out someone we love. Ten years of chasing all of the world's deepest hungers can almost ruin a life. I learned something long ago from my wife, Kris. I don't remember that Kris ever said these words, but her life speaks it: "Do what you do best and let others do what they do best." (By the way, this is very close to what the apostle Paul was getting at when he taught his churches to exercise their God-given, Spirit-shaped gifts.)

Jesus said this so well when he told some would-be disciples that kingdom dreams take priority. One man, distracted by his family, asked Jesus if he could stop following him and do something else. Jesus said, "No one who puts a hand to the plow and looks back is fit for service in the kingdom of God" (Luke 9:62).

Those are strong words; they are also true words. The focus, Jesus teaches all of us, must be to do the thing we are called to do as something swallowed up in kingdom work. Long ago I decided that God called me to be a teacher and writer; that's what I do. Some may not like my teaching and some may not like my books, but I believe that is what God called me to do and that's what I do.

In order to "do that" one thing well, one must guard from trying to do too many other things. Saying no to other things is what keeps life balanced. I've never tried to do all the following things at the same time: I've never run for office or tried to be on the school board, nor been tempted to; I've never tried to start a church and pastor a church and teach classes and also speak at churches on weekends and write books and read everyone else's books and start a magazine and edit a magazine and serve at the soup kitchen and teach a weeknight Bible study and work in the yard and plan trips to

Central America to work on orphanages ... In other words, I learned from Kris long ago to do what I do and don't do what I don't do. We have learned to keep our schedule simple.

Andy Crouch, a well-known and very smart Christian thinker, said we shouldn't try to "save the world" but we should play our part in the redemptive work of this world with a small group of friends.[64] I completely agree with Andy on this. I'd put it this way: the way to "save" the world is for everyone to do the one thing God calls them to do. When we start trying to do everything in an enthusiastic dash to save the world, we neither save the world nor do what we are called to do.

So, keep your eyes on the kingdom, make it personal, do what you do well, do only that. Now just two more things ...

IT'S OKAY TO DO ORDINARY JOBS

T. K., who works sometimes on our home, is good. I love to watch him do what God called him to do, and he's one who does just that. T. K. works with his hands. He turned our kitchen from a fifty-year-old room into a room we love, and he converted our back porch into the coolest living space we could ever imagine. When he's working at our house, I love to watch him and I don't care if I get distracted from what I do. (By the way, he's about thirty years old with the carpentry skills of a seasoned veteran.)

T. K. was born with a great artistic sense. He doesn't read books like me because God framed him to use his hands to make things. He knows Kris and me and what we like so he can take his artistic sense and match it to what we like, even when we don't know what we might like! He did the ceiling on our back porch and he began to explain what he had in mind and I had no idea what he was talking about — not the cut of the wood or the color he had in mind — so I said, "I'm not sure what you are talking about."

He said, "Don't worry, you'll like it."

To this day I can't look up at our ceiling without saying, "T. K., buddy, you got it right. We love it."

Let me ask you again about what matters. Too many think what matters is something huge and splashy and earth-shattering and world-reversing and far-off-land-saving. For many what matters must take place in a church or in a parachurch organization. But that's not true. What really matters is that you do what God made you to do, that you live that piece of God's dream that God gave to you.

LET THE KINGDOM VISION OF JESUS SWALLOW UP WHAT YOU DO

The further we get into the ordinary realities of our work, the harder it is to keep the kingdom of God in focus. So we return to our opening point but this time with a slightly different focus: *Let God's kingdom work swallow up what you do.* It's easier to be theoretical about the kingdom of God than it is to let the kingdom swallow up what you do. If the kingdom of God is about justice, love, peace, wisdom, and moral commitment, then you are summoned by God to let your life speak justice, love, peace, wisdom, and moral goodness—wherever you are and whatever you do.

But does this "do something that matters" really matter? Does it matter ultimately or to God whether or not we follow Jesus? Does it matter whether or not we take seriously his words about kingdom— justice, love, peace, wisdom, Pentecost, and give him our total life? Does it really matter?

In one word: *Yes.* For Jesus, what you do with your life matters— both now and forever.

Interlude

I was recently rereading Acts 20. The author tells us that the apostle Paul visited Ephesus (now in Turkey) on his way to Jerusalem, and Paul seemed aware that this might be the last time he'd ever get to visit one of his favorite churches and surely some of his closest friends. What did he say?

He told them that he had given everything he had to the gospel work in Ephesus and that they could look at his own track record and they would agree with him. He had preached the gospel to them and he told them they were to remember the weak. As I sat there reading the text, what forced itself on me was that Paul had no regrets over his time with the Ephesians, and so this question came to mind:

What does it take now

to live a life in which I will have no regrets

when I know my journey is near its end?

I wonder what you think of this: What kind of life do you need to have in order to say at your journey's end that you have no regrets? What kind of person do you want to be now? What kind of behaviors do you need to develop now? What kind of relationships do you want now? What kind of career do you want to choose now so that when you look back you can say: "No regrets." What kind of pursuits do you need to have now so you can end your journey as did Paul?

CHAPTER 12

ETERNITY.LIFE

I believe in heaven. I believe in heaven because Jesus did and I hope I believe in heaven *as* Jesus did. I believe in heaven because I believe in justice, in peace, and in love. I believe in heaven, in part, because of the apostles and the saints and the Reformers and Harriet Beecher Stowe and C. S. Lewis and Dorothy Sayers and Mother Teresa and the children of Rwanda. I don't, however, believe "heaven" is forever and ever. I believe that what is forever and ever is called the New Heavens and the New Earth, the time and the place where heaven comes down to earth.[65] The New Heavens and the New Earth will be the fullness of flourishing.

But belief in the New Heavens and the New Earth also means I believe in hell. I believe in hell because Jesus did. And I hope I believe in hell *as* Jesus believed in hell. I believe in hell because I believe in justice, in peace, and in love. But I don't believe hell is a gassy furnace where humans are scorched forever and ever and ever and ever, and I'll make my case below. I don't believe in Dante's hell or in God as the grand torturer. Hell will be the end of flourishing.

We live in an age when talk of hell is *verboten* and belief in hell a sign of a deranged mind and a sadistic god or goddess, and that enlightened Christians have tossed belief in hell aside. At the same time, statistics show that most people believe in life after death and that most people believe in heaven and that most people think they'll end up there.[66] I've aged enough to wonder what's on the other side and I've come to this conclusion:

if I've got One.Life,
and if there is a life after death,
and if that life is "forever and ever,"
then I want to live now in light of the longer stretch of life.

Ignoring eternity is foolish. Living in light of eternity is wisdom.

But, yes, there are some people who focus too much on the future and not enough on now. As Miss Maudie, that wonderful character in Harper Lee's profound *To Kill a Mockingbird*, puts it: "Those are just some kind of men who—who're so busy worrying about the next world they've never learned to live in this one, and you can look down the street and see the results."[67] But the lopsidedness of some is not cured by a reactionary lopsidedness, and that is why Jesus taught us to pray for God's will to be done "on earth as it is in heaven." The wise learn to live *now* but to do so *in the light of eternity.*

Let's take the negative side of eternity first.

JESUS BELIEVED IN HELL

Once I stood between an Old Testament scholar and a passionate young woman who made this bold claim to the scholar: "I don't believe in the God of the Old Testament. That God is full of wrath and judgment and hell. The God of the New Testament, however, is full of grace and truth and love and peace. We Christians believe in the New Testament God." Having unloaded on the scholar, she thought she had made her point and was ready now to move on to finer and better ideas. Case closed. Except the scholar had pondered this view. The Old Testament scholar paused, looked her in the eyes, and said in short staccato sentences,

"The God of the Old Testament is Jesus' God.
"Jesus talks more about hell than anyone in the Bible.
"The Old Testament never mentions hell as we know it now.
"The God of the Old Testament is full of grace and
    compassion."

The conversation ended as I recall. But what the scholar said thoroughly impressed me, and I'd like anyone who considers following Jesus to consider what Jesus says about the negative stretch of the afterlife. He isn't shy about what happens after we die. Followers of Jesus also follow Jesus in what he believes, in what he believes about what happens when we die.

So what did Jesus say? His kingdom dream was primarily shaped by a glorious vision of the New Heavens and New Earth, but also by a hell, and the following words make this abundantly clear:

> Enter through the narrow gate. For wide is the gate and broad is the road that leads to **destruction**, and many enter through it. But small is the gate and narrow the road that leads to **life**, and only a few find it.
>
> *Matthew 7:13–14*

> Every tree that does not bear good fruit is cut down and thrown into the **fire**.
>
> *Matthew 7:19*

> Do not be afraid of those who kill the body but cannot kill the soul. Rather, be afraid of the One who can destroy both soul and body in **hell**.
>
> *Matthew 10:28*

> Whoever publicly acknowledges me I will also **acknowledge** before my Father in heaven. But whoever publicly disowns me I will **disown** before my Father in heaven.
>
> *Matthew 10:32–33*

> If your hand or your foot causes you to stumble, cut it off and throw it away. It is better for you to enter **life** maimed or crippled than to have two hands or two feet and be thrown into **eternal fire**. And if your eye causes you to stumble, gouge it out and throw it away. It is better for you to enter **life** with one eye than to have two eyes and be thrown into the **fire of hell**.
>
> *Matthew 18:8–9*

> Then he will say to those on his left, "Depart from me, you who are cursed, into the **eternal fire** prepared for the devil and his angels."
>
> *Matthew 25:41*

Jesus clearly believed *that* there was life after death and he clearly believed in what I want to call "*death after death*" too. In short, Jesus believed that after we die we will meet our Maker and will have to account for whether or not we entered the narrow gate, bore good fruit, acknowledged Jesus publicly, and lived good lives that treated the marginalized with compassion. Jesus believed that our Maker will assign us to one of two places: the life place or the death place. I believe in "death after death" because Jesus taught it. Perhaps it is wiser to say that since Jesus believed in hell, his followers follow him in that conviction. Again, Jesus believed those who didn't follow him, who rejected God's ways and who oppressed others and who waged war against peace and who were unloving and who were foolish in this life would not inherit the kingdom of God and would experience a final endless death after physical death. The scheme would be something like this: we are born, we live, we die, we are raised to judgment, we are judged to death after death. Death after death is awful to consider, but it's extremely foolish not to consider.

Justice, too, demands some kind of belief in final death after death. If there is any theme that drives the future dream of the Bible it is that on that Day God will finally establish justice. The wonderful song of Mary in Luke 1, called the Magnificat, sings just that note:

> He has brought down rulers from their thrones
> but has lifted up the humble.
> He has filled the hungry with good things
> but has sent the rich away empty.

From Moses to the prophets, from Jesus to the end of the Book of Revelation, this theme is clear: though injustice may haunt our world right now and though we may experience horrific tragedies in the here and now, the overriding hope is that *someday justice will finally be established*. Our dreams of fairness and our dreams for justice are anchored in this hope that someday God will make all things right. The kingdom dream of Jesus opens up to us a revelation of God's final future: "may your will be done on earth as it is in heaven." That yearning is why I have to believe that injustice and death will not have the final world; someday justice will be established.

Any talk about eternity leads to curiosity about who's in and who's out. Some use stereotypes to make their points. As New Testament scholar Dale Allison put it, "I do not know what befell Mother Teresa of Calcutta when she died, nor what has become of Joseph Stalin. But the same thing cannot have come upon both."[68] When another New Testament professor posted that very quotation of Allison on my blog, a scientist friend ("RJS") wrote this: "but on the other hand if there is any moral rhyme or reason in the universe, the same thing cannot happen to Stalin and the 10 year-old who died of pneumonia in Tibet a thousand years ago." Naming names won't get us very far and frankly puts us too close to the judgment seat. Which leads me to a set of convictions I've had for decades:

> God is the Judge, and we're not.
> What God judges will be brilliant justice but
> God's justice will be soaked in God's own grace.
> I hope for a final day of overwhelming grace
> that swallows up all sin and injustice.

But Jesus' own teachings lead me to see a final "death after death."

What will it be like (according to Jesus)?

What will this "death after death" be like? We need to get something clear first. The Greek word *Gehenna* stands behind the Bible's use of the word *hell*.[69] But *Gehenna* is a proper name of a valley south of Jerusalem, notorious for a place where child sacrifice and pagan worship occurred. Representing the place where the worst of sins were committed, the prophets announced Gehenna would be the (metaphorical or not) place of God's judgment, and the place was connected to death and unquenchable fire and worms eventually devouring everything. Gehenna, or hell, this notorious place of fire and judgment, becomes for Jesus and his followers a metaphor for God's final judgment.

But this leads the inquiring mind to ask what hell, or death after death, will really be like. If Gehenna is a metaphor, what's it a metaphor for? Are we to imagine "death after death" as a real fire that never goes out? As both a place of darkness and fire, and also a grave where worms eat away? We are safest to unpack the imagery and avoid the overly graphic, something many have not been able to do, including Dante in his famous *Inferno*. *Hell* then represents the place of judgment, a word used to describe "death after death," but at the same time—and perhaps even more importantly—the imagery Jesus uses functions rhetorically to awaken the conscience to God's call to repent. Jesus spoke this way in order to awaken people to turn from sin and turn to God.

PROBLEMS WITH HELL

An increasing number of people find hell, or eternal conscious punishment, to be an intolerable notion, and such persons cannot believe a God of grace and love could ever punish humans endlessly in what they often call, to ramp up their argument, God's torture chamber. At the other end of the spectrum, and probably the minority today, others think of hell as a place of pain and misery that goes on endlessly and endlessly and endlessly for humans who are also endlessly and endlessly conscious. Many find a fundamental injustice at work in this view of hell. Here's a consideration that I can't shake (though I could be wrong): one cannot justly, and I emphasize "justly," be punished eternally for temporal sins. That is, the sins humans commit now, regardless of how vile, last less than a hundred years, and it is hard to imagine an eternal, endless, infinite punishment for a finite amount of sinning. Eventually justice should be served. Eventually all the sins and sinfulness would get their due. We must learn to think about such matters rationally. Any parent who locked up a child in a closet for fifteen years for swiping a cookie would be considered a monster, and it follows that we must correlate punishment with sin if we are to be consistent in what we mean by justice. So a third way has been attractive to some: Without denying a belief in hell, many Christians today argue that *eternal* hell for *temporal* sins amounts to injustice and have come to believe in "conditional immortality" or "annihilationism."[70] That is, they believe immortality is only for the followers of Jesus while those who reject Jesus will be raised to judgment, experience a final justice, but eventually disappear into non-existence—that is, into an unconscious death after death. We ought to avoid dogmatism here, but I agree that God punishing humans eternally for a finite number of sins seems to be an intolerable injustice and unworthy of how the Bible talks about our just God.

So where are we? I have thought long and hard about hell and have come to a view that modifies the second view above: *hell is a person's awareness of being utterly absent, which is what "death after death" means, but yet in the presence of God,* like C. S. Lewis' wraiths yearning to be observed and present but deeply aware that they have declined both options.[71] I am unconvinced that annihilation fully answers all that Jesus says, but I also believe the second view doesn't contain enough mercy and grace.

One thing, though, is quite clear to me: Jesus believed that death would lead us into the presence of God to receive what is just from a God who is utterly gracious and utterly just. There were two options in his view of judgment: death after death or life after death. Jesus warned of the former and promised the latter.

And he spoke like this to awaken people to follow him and to know that what we do now and what we decide now matter—forever.

JESUS BELIEVED IN THE NEW HEAVENS AND THE NEW EARTH

Heaven in the mind of most is the eternal life place. Most of us believe that when we die we go to heaven, and we also believe that heaven is our eternal dwelling place. Whether we think we'll be flitting around like angels and playing harps and jutting here and there in some ethereal existence, or instead carrying on with new abilities and in perfect form can all be set aside for the moment. Recent studies have asked Bible readers to be more precise about what the eternal home for Jesus' followers will be like. On the basis of what the New Testament does say, the final home should not be called "heaven" but instead the "new heavens and the new earth," and this makes a significant difference for understanding that what we do now really does matter—for we will continue doing it on the other side of life after death. (I hope at some time you can read J. R. R. Tolkien's brilliant short story called "Leaf by Niggle," because I can think of no better description of the continuity of this life in the New Heavens and the New Earth.)

Jesus prophesied a future kingdom, the dream kingdom come true, and he fashioned it most often as a banquet in a city. The climactic revelation in the book of Revelation concerns a City, the New Jerusalem, and this Eternal City descends from the heavens down to earth so that it is the meeting place of heaven and earth. The single most important implication is this: if the final state is the New Heavens and the New Earth, and the New Heavens and New Earth are a City on a transformed earth, then the eternal state is the *perfection of life on earth and not an escape from life on earth.*

This City embodies the vision of Isaiah 60, mentioned earlier, where the governor will be Shalom and the walls of the City called Salvation and that City's gates called Praise. This City embodies everything Jesus spoke of when he dreamed of God's kingdom. A careful reading of this chapter in Revelation, because it is so earthly and realistic, suggests we should envision the New Heavens and the New Earth as a place with golf courses and parking lots and gardens and homes and coffee shops and families and friends and parties and concerts and sports and authors still writing good books—and better than we've read yet—and businesspeople doing wonderful business with others … all done right and well and with justice and peace and wisdom and perfect love in all directions by people totally devoted to God and to others.

Here's how the climactic scene in Revelation describes what we most often call "heaven," and I quote the whole chapter because I fear we don't pay enough attention to it. When we do, we see what the eternal looks like:

> Rev. 21:1 Then I saw "**a new heaven and a new earth**," for the first heaven and the first earth had passed away, and there was no longer any sea. 2 I saw the **Holy City, the new Jerusalem**, coming down out of heaven from God, prepared as a bride beautifully dressed for her husband. 3 And I heard a loud voice from the throne saying, "Look! God's dwelling place is now among the people, and he will dwell with them. They will be his people, and God himself will be with them and be their God. 4 'He will wipe every tear from their eyes. There will be no more death' or mourning or crying or pain, for the old order of things has passed away."

5 He who was seated on the throne said, "I am making every-thing new!" Then he said, "Write this down, for these words are trustworthy and true."

6 He said to me: "It is done. I am the Alpha and the Omega, the Beginning and the End. To the thirsty I will give water without cost from the spring of the water of life. 7 Those who are victorious will inherit all this, and I will be their God and they will be my children. 8 But the cowardly, the unbelieving, the vile, the mur-derers, the sexually immoral, those who practice magic arts, the idolaters and all liars — they will be consigned to the fiery lake of burning sulfur. This is the second death."

9 One of the seven angels who had the seven bowls full of the seven last plagues came and said to me, "Come, I will show you the bride, the wife of the Lamb." 10 And he carried me away in the Spirit to a mountain great and high, and showed me the **Holy City, Jerusalem**, coming down out of heaven from God. 11 It shone with the glory of God, and its brilliance was like that of a very precious jewel, like a jasper, clear as crystal. 12 It had a great, high wall with twelve gates, and with twelve angels at the gates. On the gates were written the names of the twelve tribes of Israel. 13 There were three gates on the east, three on the north, three on the south and three on the west. 14 The wall of the city had twelve foundations, and on them were the names of the twelve apostles of the Lamb.

15 The angel who talked with me had a measuring rod of gold to measure the city, its gates and its walls. 16 The city was laid out like a square, as long as it was wide. He measured the city with the rod and found it to be 12,000 stadia in length, and as wide and high as it is long. 17 He measured its wall and it was 144 cubits thick, by human measurement, which the angel was using. 18 The wall was made of jasper, and the city of pure gold, as pure as glass. 19 The foundations of the city walls were decorated with every kind of precious stone. The first foundation was jasper, the second sapphire, the third agate, the fourth emerald, 20 the fifth onyx, the sixth ruby, the seventh chrysolite, the eighth beryl, the ninth topaz, the tenth turquoise, the eleventh jacinth, and the twelfth amethyst. 21 The twelve gates were twelve pearls, each gate made of a single pearl. The great street of the city was of gold, as pure as transparent glass.

22 **I did not see a temple in the city, because the Lord God Almighty and the Lamb are its temple**. 23 The city does not

need the sun or the moon to shine on it, for the glory of God gives it light, and the Lamb is its lamp. 24 The nations will walk by its light, and the kings of the earth will bring their splendor into it. 25 On no day will its gates ever be shut, for there will be no night there. 26 The glory and honor of the nations will be brought into it. 27 Nothing impure will ever enter it, nor will anyone who does what is shameful or deceitful, but only those whose names are written in the Lamb's book of life.

This New Jerusalem — on earth as it is in heaven — is justice, and it is peace, and it is love, and it is wisdom, and it involves everyone loving God and others with every globule of their being in an endless exploration of the Life God wants of each one of us. The New Jerusalem — on earth as it is in heaven — is the dream kingdom of Jesus in its finality and perfection and glory.

> The people of God,
> living with God,
> and living with one another in perfect shalom and love and
> justice.

Everyone will be in direct contact with God and the Lamb, whose death brought forgiveness and redemption and liberation — hence no temple.

So when Jesus says "kingdom" and he teaches us to dream of that kingdom by praying for that kingdom in the Lord's Prayer, this vision in Revelation 21 is what he has in mind. In the meantime, his followers are seeking to live out that kind of kingdom in the here and now.

So, how is heaven best defined? Let me reverse the terms of our definition of hell: heaven is *a person's awareness and overwhelming delight in being absolutely present in the utter presence of God.* That is, the New Heavens and the New Earth is the final state of living with God in God's world as God made it to be.

Interlude

What are the first five words that come to mind when you hear the word *hell*? What are the first five words that come to mind when you hear *heaven*? What do you believe about hell and heaven? How close are your views to what Jesus taught?

This question has been in my head since I was a college student: Why did Jesus talk so much about the future kingdom and a future hell? It is too easy to think Jesus was the good guy and some of those Old Testament prophets, or Moses, were the crusty guys who saw God as full of wrath and "the Judge." What is not easy for many of us to get our head around is how much Jesus said about hell. Why do you think Jesus talked like this? Why did the Good Guy talk about the Good Place and the Bad Place so much?

A recent analysis of what Americans believe revealed that Americans think about 70 percent of people will go to heaven. Which means most Americans think most people will go to heaven. Do you agree or disagree? How do you think Jesus would answer the question: Who will go to heaven when they die?

That same study revealed that 73 percent of Americans believe in hell while 82 percent believe in heaven. Are you surprised that nearly three-quarters of Americans believe in hell? Why do you think the topic, then, is so sensitive?

Here's a wise question to ponder: If your life has two parts, the earthly part (that lasts about seventy or eighty years) and an eternity part (that lasts forever), which part should have the greatest influence on how you live? How should that eternity part influence the earthly part?

Interlude

CHAPTER 13

GOD IS LOVE LIFE

At the center of Jesus' dream is God, and there is yet another element of his dream we have not yet discussed. The God at the very center of Jesus' dream, the God who makes an appearance in Jesus' parables, the God who took on flesh and became human, is a God of love. Lots of people say they know *that* God loves them, but deep inside they don't feel loved and so they feel like impostors with God. Even more, deep inside they are so conflicted about love itself that they cannot become vulnerable enough to embrace this God and know that God embraces back.

> It is much easier to say we believe God loves us than
> it is to bask and dwell in that God of Love
> by receiving and returning love.

Until we get back to Before Time, until we get to the Middle of All Things, and until we get our heart connected to God's heart, Jesus' dream kingdom will be neither understood nor embraced. At the core of Jesus' dream kingdom is God, and that God is a God of Love. No, even better, that God *is* Love the way that God *is* Life.

But not all of us imagine God this way and not all of us love God or are convinced God really loves us. There are, in fact, four gods that reside in the brains of Americans.[72] "Whether we are conscious of it or not, we all assign a personality to God." Fair enough. But Andrew Newberg, a neuroscientist who specializes in the brain and religion, goes on to explain that the personality we assign to God

"... appears to be neurologically based on the nature of our own personality."

So what are these four gods according to Newberg?

- The authoritarian god (32% of us)
- The critical god (16% of us)
- The distant god (24% of us)
- The benevolent god (23% of us)

The authoritarian/critical god(s) activate one part of our brain (the fear part, called the limbic areas) while the benevolent God activates another part (the prefrontal cortex). Our view of God and our view of kingdom are intertwined. If we have a limbic-area-only god, then we also will have a limbic-area kingdom — and that means one shaped by fear and authority and judgment and sword and violence and wars. If we have a prefrontal-cortex-area god, then we will also have a prefrontal-cortex kingdom — and that means one shaped by love and benevolence and peace and compassion.

Followers of Jesus, though, don't get to choose whether they want a limbic-system god or a prefrontal-cortex god. Instead, followers of Jesus assume the habit of asking Jesus what he thinks, and the one thing that seems evident to the whole of the Christian tradition is that the God of the Bible, the God of Jesus, whom Jesus calls *Abba*, is a limbic-*and*-prefrontal-cortex God who is both inflexibly holy and at the same time wildly gracious and loving. Through the limbic and prefrontal cortex areas God produces a both-sides-of-the-brain kingdom.

If it is accurate to say that only 23 percent of Americans affirm a loving/benevolent god, while almost half believe in an authoritarian/critical god and another quarter finds god distant, we are in serious need of revisiting the origins of what Jesus and the Christian faith teach about God — especially if we want to embrace the full dream of Jesus for the kingdom.

We need to think back into Time and Before Time to the time when God was all there was, back to Before this world of ours even existed. What we have learned from Jesus and the New Testament and the Church is that God was *perichoreting*. That is, God was indwelling God. The Father. The Son. The Spirit. One. Three-in-One. Indwelling and interpenetrating One Another in the endless God Dance of love and delight. This dance of love is who God was and is, and this is what God is like and what God will always be like, and that means that the only way to be connected to God is to love the God who is Love himself.

To follow Jesus into this God-who-is-Love God is to enter into the Divine Dance. Jesus' vision of the dream kingdom, then, is a dream about dancing with the God who *is* Love. It's like Jesus to imagine a world where that kind of God was at work. So we must listen to another of Jesus' stories and ...

IMAGINE A WORLD WHERE GOD IS LOVE

Jesus was imagining the kingdom one day when he told a parable we call the Prodigal Son. Context is so important for this parable. The story starts at a table where Jesus is dining with the religious experts of Jesus' day who had serious questions about his table friends:

> *Now the tax collectors and "sinners" were all gathering around to hear Jesus. But the Pharisees and the teachers of the law muttered, "This man welcomes sinners and eats with them."*
>
> *Luke 15:1–2*

The experts want Jesus to explain himself for doing such an unholy thing like associating with (to the point of sharing a meal with) sinners. Jesus does explain himself, but he does so by telling a fantastic story that takes their question and sabotages it. At the same time, the tax collectors and sinners are listening in to Jesus' response and they discover that he is tossing grace toward them.

Jesus' parable is about a father, about an older son, and a younger son. The younger son wanders off into a life of sin and the older son sticks to the backyard and plays the part of a good Torah-observant son. Both boys depict paths that squander their One.Life into death, the first because it is sensually selfish, the second because it is full of pride and presumption.

The older boy is like the person today who grows up in a good Christian home, goes off to college, avoids the party scene, keeps his pants on when he's alone with his girlfriend, graduates with good grades, and takes a job in his father's firm. The younger boy also grows up in a Christian home, goes off to college, and decides to drink hard and smoke pot and get in bed with as many girls as he can. He fiddle-faddles his grades away, graduates due to grade inflation, wanders from job to job and shacks with friends and sometimes with a girl and, after about ten years, wakes up one morning, looks in the mirror and sees a fool.

"What's a father to do?" his listeners must have asked.

"Not what you think," Jesus reveals.

WHO'S YOUR FATHER?

Jesus invites us to enter into a dream world in this parable. When we do, we find ourselves in a new world, a world Jesus calls "the kingdom of God." What Jesus wants us to see in this Kingdom.Life is a Father-God who loves us in ways we never imagined and a table of fellowship that is full of Kingdom.Life joy and love. But this father sabotages the expectations of many listeners (and many today are like them).

First, when the younger son asks for his share of the estate we're led to believe the father had to sell off one-third of his property. The younger son wanted what his father had without wanting to love his father in an enduring, loyal relationship. Or, as Tim Keller, a pastor in Manhattan, puts it: "He wanted his father's things, but not his father."[73]

Your response is the same as mine: "The kid's a creep!" The astounding thing is that the father does what the son wants. This father does not coerce love and grants his son freedom to be who he wants to be.

As we enter deeper into this parabolic world of Jesus we listen to a father who spots his boy returning from a far-off distance and ... well, Jesus' words are better than mine:

> But while he was still a long way off, his father saw him and was filled with compassion for him; he ran to his son, threw his arms around him and kissed him.

v. 20

Nothing the father does here is expected in that Jewish culture. Fathers didn't wait for rebellious sons to come home; they didn't respond to returning rebels by running as fast as they could to meet the son; they didn't welcome them home. They disciplined them and perhaps even banned them from returning ever again. Fathers didn't do these things, but this father does. Jesus tells this story for you and me to see how incredibly lavish the father's love is for his son, and to sketch before our watching eyes the lavish love of God for those who have done far more bad things than their conscience can control.

When the son comes clean with the father about all his sick behaviors, which are nothing more than day-by-day rejections of his father's love, his family's relationships, and their daily fellowship, the father throws a huge party—giving his son his own robe and his ring and some solid sandals, and then feasting over a prime-quality fattened calf (think stacks of Omaha Steaks), and all the while playing music for singing and dancing and making merry. This is Dickens-like merriment.

The older son . . . what about him?

WHO'S NAKED NOW?

Just before this parable closes down its shutters for the day, Jesus escorts us into a world where those who think they are religious experts are really naked (and ugly), like the unsuspecting emperor in the story called "The Emperor's New Clothes."

> Meanwhile, the older son was in the field. When he came near the house, he heard music and dancing. So he called one of the servants and asked him what was going on. "Your brother has come," he replied, "and your father has killed the fattened calf because he has him back safe and sound."
>
> The older brother became angry and refused to go in. So his father went out and pleaded with him. But he answered his father, "Look! All these years I've been slaving for you and never disobeyed your orders. Yet you never gave me even a young goat so I could celebrate with my friends. But when this son of yours who has squandered your property with prostitutes comes home, you kill the fattened calf for him!"
>
> *Luke 15:25–30*

Jesus knew the religious experts were the biggest opponents to God's kingdom world, where God's love and grace and peace and justice would flow like the Niagara Falls. So he holds them up in almost comic relief in this parable. (Well, if it weren't so serious it would be comic relief.) Instead, he makes them tragic figures, people who think they are on the inside but whose hearts are so full of pride and presumption (of the father's love and joy) they find themselves—painfully and embarrassingly—outside griping instead of inside partying with the father and his younger son.

Every time I read this story—and I tell this as a confession—I feel a little triumphant over the older son. I find that it's all too easy to point fingers at the older son and pretend I am not like him. The irony of this parabolic world of Jesus is that *finger pointing shows we are the older son.* The "good guy" in this story is the "sinner guy"—the sinner guy who sins bad, who comes to his senses with sorrow, and who returns home in repentance. It is the sinner guy who becomes the reason for the party. But the sinner guy is not the good guy because of his sin. He is the good guy because he comes clean before the father (God). Most notably, the posture of the younger son is one of sorrow, repentance, humility, and utter delight in getting to be back home with the father. It's scary to be the younger son in this story because it means we have come clean before God, before a father who stands at the estate's edge praying we will come home and sit at his table today. It's scary because we have to meet the father at the gate and we have to walk that road back to the home with the father and we have to listen to him take the heat for letting us back in before everyone else could condemn us for our horrid behaviors.

We've got to imagine this world to make it happen. The dream of reconciliation with God and with the family can only happen if we first believe it can, and then we have to take the first steps to return to the Father.

WHO'S WEARING THE FANCY CLOTHES?

So, if we want to be in the party (the kingdom), we've got to imagine that we stand with the younger son. The parable tells the story of a young rebel who wanders into a life of ruin and sin, and nothing typifies this more for Jesus' Jewish audience than telling us that the younger boy was feeding pigs and yearning to eat pig slop.

> So he went and hired himself out to a citizen of that country, who sent him to his fields to feed pigs. He longed to fill his stomach with the pods that the pigs were eating, but no one gave him anything.
>
> *Luke 15:15–16*

I like that last line and I think it gratifies the older son and his companions. No one gave him anything ... and we can just hear the murmurs, "And he deserved his hunger!" It reminds me of the gossips and ever-present eyes that haunted Hester Prynne in *The Scarlet Letter*.

In the young son's condition, after years of wasting his (father's well-earned and respectable) money and after running his dopamine levels to record highs, he came to his senses. It is this contrast that makes this parable so powerful: a ruined and deformed character figures it out and God is waiting there for him and ushers him into the perichoretic dance of joy and life and love.

What the young man figured out though is profoundly insightful. He doesn't just say: "I am so stupid!" or "My bad!" or "I've wasted all this money!" Notice how deep this young man goes into the long inner-defeat of repentance and self-discovery:

> When he came to his senses, he said, "How many of my father's hired servants have food to spare, and here I am starving to death! I will set out and go back to my father and say to him: Father, I have sinned against heaven and against you. I am no longer worthy to be called your son; make me like one of your hired servants." So he got up and went to his father.
>
> But while he was still a long way off, his father saw him and was filled with compassion for him; he ran to his son, threw his arms around him and kissed him.
>
> The son said to him, "Father, I have sinned against heaven and against you. I am no longer worthy to be called your son."
>
> *Luke 15:17–21*

This is where God's love gets serious. After years of rebellion and ruining his life, the younger son—with his back in the corner of a pigsty and shame flooding his soul and his arrogance now broken in half—admits what he has done and whom he has offended. The Kingdom.Life can't be found until we tell the truth about ourselves both to ourselves and to our God.

It is too easy to think we can just stop our sinning. Or perhaps we are tempted to appeal to the solidarity theme. That is, to admit our sin by saying: "We are *all* sinful. We *all* fail. We're *all* alike." The implication, of course, is: "*I'm* not so bad after all." But the younger son goes one step further and enters into the embrace of his father by telling the deeper truth about himself: "I have sinned against heaven [God] and against you [his father]." This confession gets beyond solidarity with others into the solitary zone; he makes it doubly personal. *He* has sinned and he has sinned against *God* and his *father*, both of whom are persons whose love he risked in his rebellion. In other words, real confession admits more than that we have done something wrong (like I have stolen or I have lied or I have cheated). Real confession, *true* confession, admits that *I* have done something to *someone else*. True confession admits that I walked away from God's Dance, and true confession asks God to walk me back to the dance floor.

God waits and God will usher us back.

God.Is.Love.

IMAGINE THAT KIND OF WORLD

Jesus' parable imagines the kind of world where truth-telling persons sit down with other truth-telling persons in a society with no masks. These kingdom persons know who they are, what they have done, what they have done before God, and who they are before God. Instead of walking away from the Waiting and Forgiving Father, they own up to what they have done, walk home, and become *vulnerable* to the response of God.

The message of Jesus is that . . .

God is waiting

God will accept you

God will throw a party in the heavenly courts

When you tell the truth about yourself
To yourself and to God

The kingdom dream of Jesus is designed for those who will tell the truth about themselves, turn from their sins, and turn back to God by banking on God's gracious forgiveness in Jesus' death and resurrection, God's gracious welcome, and the open seat waiting at the table in God's family.

Interlude

How did you respond to the idea about the personalities Americans have assigned to God? Where would you classify yourself? Do you think God is ...

- The authoritarian god (32% of us)
- The critical god (16% of us)
- The distant god (24% of us)
- The benevolent god (23% of us)

Why do you think so many of us affirm and confess that God is Love but have such a hard time embracing the God who is Love and knowing the God who is Love actually loves us?

What is love? C. S. Lewis, in his book *The Four Loves*, famously distinguished between four kinds of love (affection, friendship, eros, and charity). I sometimes have defined love like this:

Love of God is to yearn for, strive for, and work for whatever glorifies God as we dwell with God as intimately as possible. Love of others means to yearn for, strive for, and work for whatever God wants for another person.

But ...

I've come to a simpler way of saying this, and it gives me a better handle on what it means to say God loves us:

Love is being "with" as a "for."

That is, love is a commitment to be "with" someone

but to be with that someone as a person who is "for" that person.

This is exactly what the covenant of the Old Testament (look it up in Genesis 12, 15, 17, 22; and then Exodus 19–24) is about. God says he enters into a relationship with us like this: "I will be your God and you will be my people." That is, God will be with us and he will be for us in order to make us what God wants us to be. God's love for us then is "being 'with' us as the One who is 'for' us."

What can you do — today — to actualize your beliefs that God is Love and that God loves you?

CHAPTER 14

CROSS LIFE
RESURRECTION LIFE

You can start with Moses or you can start with any of Israel's prophets, from Obadiah to Malachi, and their favorite way to call Israel to its senses and back to the Kingdom.Life was to tell them: "Repent!" When they used the word *repent*, or in Hebrew *shuv*, they were using a picture, the picture of someone turning around 180 degrees and walking the opposite direction. Too many people think repenting means feeling terrible about something someone has done. Feeling bad is fine, and it often accompanies repentance, but repentance is not so much about what we feel but the twofold prong of owning up to our own injustices and failures to love, and starting all over by living justly and lovingly.

Most importantly, *shuv* is not what you say and it's more than saying sorry. Think about it: You don't care if your friend says she's sorry; you want her to quit talking about you behind your back. Not until she ceases from her gossip can you trust her again, and not until she stops and begins using her tongue lovingly will your friendship be right. *Shuv* means real changes, and Christianity needs to get this right once again.

Repentance means real behavioral changes.

That's how John the Baptist saw things too. In one episode in his life, he opened up a public address with some strong words for the religulous leaders of his day. He flat-out called them a den of snakes.

(Imagine some raised eyebrows and some heartbeats increasing and some intense gazing at one another.) Their response was to appeal to their privilege as God's people, that God had elected Israel. (It's heating up now.)

John's response? Pointing down at the rocks on the ground, he countered: "Out of these stones God can raise up children for Abraham." (John doesn't back down and pull a Mr. Rogers softener out for them.) John cranks it up a notch and warns them that if they don't respond, God will judge the nation. Here John is predicting what would happen in AD 70 when the Romans would sack Jerusalem and destroy the temple. This was a face-to-face showdown between prophet and leaders, the sort of thing that happened over and over in Israel's history.

Wow, the ordinary Jew who was at the scene was probably thinking, "If this is what the leaders need to do in order to repent, what should we do then?"

Here is where John reveals that repentance is more than feeling sorry and saying you're sorry. John's idea of *shuv* alters life from the inside out. Read these words carefully because this is what real repentance is:

> Anyone who has two shirts should share with the one who has none, and anyone who has food should do the same.
>
> *Luke 3:11*

Genuine *shuv*-ing means concrete acts of justice that result in distributing clothing and food. Tax collectors were told not to collect any more than they were required to, which would end the economic violence they were unjustly inflicting on hardworking farmers and artisans. Soldiers, too, approached John and asked what *shuv* looked like for them:

> Don't extort money and don't accuse people falsely—be content with your pay.
>
> *Luke 3:14*

It is too easy to think we've got this *shuv* thing down and done and let's get on with the good things. It's too easy to think that feeling guilty about sin and about our complicity in the world's injustices is the point of repentance, and I think some like to feel bad about their complicity in injustice. It's too easy to confuse saying we're sorry to God or feeling bad with real repentance. But not for the prophets or for John or for Jesus.

> *Shuv* means concrete, real-life changes
> **from** unjust actions and unpeaceful deeds and unloving behaviors
> **into** the Kingdom.Life of acts of justice, deeds shaped by peace, and behaviors that reveal God's love.

Now we need to get to the heart of it all for Jesus, because Jesus sums all this up—everything we are to do—with one image: the cross.

JESUS AND THE UNDESERVED CROSS

> Jesus,
> though Son of God,
> though Messiah,
> though a Galilean benefactor,
> though a teacher of wisdom,
> though a prophet,
> though righteous,
> though compassionate and loving,
> though a good man,
> though a favorite of the people,
> though steeped in Israel's scriptures,
> though aware of Israel's traditions,
> though hailed by crowds,
> though accompanied by followers,
> though in the City of David,
> though staring at the seat of justice in Jerusalem,
> though examined by the highest of authorities,
> though capable of giving profound answers to life's questions,
> though responding to unjust accusations with grace,
> though ... though ... though ... all these things and many more ...

… Was condemned to capital punishment and unjustly and publicly crucified at Golgotha. He was like an innocent lamb led to a slaughter, and the prophet Isaiah predicted that very thing about the Messiah (Isaiah 52–53). As the sun was eclipsed, so was justice. The darkness of the scene was the darkness of injustice. They chose to put him away, this Lamb of God, with the ultimate punishment: crucifixion.

Crucifixion is the ultimate obscenity.
Crucifixion is the ultimate deterrent.
Crucifixion involves stripping the victim in order to humiliate.
Crucifixion means a body would be picked apart by birds of
   prey.
Crucifixion sates the sadistic desires of the strong.
Crucifixion is reserved for vile criminals.
Crucifixion is synonymous with shame.
Crucifixion is synonymous with suffocation.
Crucifixion gives a lasting commentary on a person's life.
Crucifixion means a person is cursed by God.

Those who were lined up for the kingdom dream of Jesus since his days in Galilee could not believe what happened at Golgotha. In Galilee he was a Jewish prophet who convinced many that the kingdom of God was already at work. In Galilee he performed deeds that showed he was in tune with God. In Galilee he opened up the Kingdom.Life for thousands. In Galilee he created tables of fellowship and tables of joy. In Galilee the most ostracized persons in society found their way to God. In Galilee people sensed the kingdom of God was on the horizon and coming their way.

But in Golgotha everything was destroyed. Or so it looked like everything was destroyed. Three days later Jesus was raised, and the cross morphed from an instrument of injustice into the place of grace. The cross, where Jesus bore the pain and sins of others, became both a place of redemptive power and a model for discipleship. Our sins morph into his, our death morphs into his, and our stories morph into his. And at the very same time his righteousness morphs into ours, his life morphs into ours, and his story morphs into our story.

Perhaps we forget something here. Jesus has entered into your suffering and into your disgraces and into your depressions and into your shames and into your pains. The cross is not just a redemptive place for the follower of Jesus. The cross is also the solidarity place where God joined us in our deepest death. Perhaps you've lost a friend who got drunk and then had a fatal car accident, or perhaps you've lost the joy of family togetherness because of divorce, or perhaps you've seen a friend waste away from some disease, or perhaps you've got a tattoo on your body that evokes bad memories. The cross is about that, too.

At the cross Jesus enters into our pain, into our tragedies, into our injustices, and into the systemic evil we have created and into the sins we have ourselves committed. But his solidarity with us is also an act of redemption.

> Galilee morphs into Golgotha, and Golgotha morphs into
> Grace.
> His Golgotha morphs into our Golgotha,
> and his Golgotha morphs into our Grace.
> Our One.Life becomes His.Life as His.Life becomes Our.Life.
> If we embrace Jesus, we embrace the Jesus of the Cross.
> To embrace the Jesus of the Cross is to die through shuving.

THE LAMB AND HIS LAMBS

The deeper our experience of our own need of shuv (repentant dying), the more we embrace the potent words of Jesus that following him means going to the cross every day of our life. "Whoever wants to be my disciple must deny themselves and take up their cross daily and follow me" (Luke 9:23). There are four lines here and they form a poetic set of lines called a chiasm, the repetition of items in reverse order — as in "ABBA," a Swedish rock group of my vintage. The four lines of Jesus can be schematically listed like this:

> A Be my disciple
>   B Deny themselves
>   B Take up their cross daily
> A Follow me.

Being a disciple and following Jesus belong together just as do denying self and taking up the cross daily. Theologians sometimes call this way of framing the ethical life a "cruciform" life. If the Son of God, the Messiah, was the Lamb of God, his followers are to become self-sacrificing lambs of God as well. If the Cross of the Messiah marks us, we become lambs like the Messiah.

I wonder if you have ever paid attention to two things about churches and Christian art: first, there are crosses everywhere; second, there are all kinds of crosses.[74] Some crosses have Jesus hanging on them (crucifixes); some have an empty cross. Some crosses cross in the middle, some in the upper portion, and some at the top (called the Tau cross). You can find crosses on mountaintops and in valleys, you can find them around someone's neck and you can find them marked on suitcases and tattooed on bodies. Some crosses are kitschy while others are profound. The Egyptians have a special design, the Celts have a special design, the Huegenots have a special design, shepherds have a cross, the Roman Catholics have a cross, and the Orthodox have a cross ... I could go on. The cross is at the center of the Christian Church and always has been. Truly, following Jesus and believing in Jesus are about a cross-shaped life, a life that offers itself in every dimension of life as a lamb on the altar of God.

My favorite theologian is a German: his name is Dietrich Bonhoeffer. He gave his life for the gospel. An English officer, Payne Best, who was also imprisoned during World War II, said this of Bonhoeffer's character:

> He was one of the very few persons I have ever met for whom God was real and always near.... On Sunday, April 8, 1945, Pastor Bonhoeffer conducted a little service of worship ... He found just the right words to express the spirit of our imprisonment ... He had hardly ended his last prayer when the door opened and two civilians entered. They said, 'Prisoner Bonhoeffer, come with us.' That had only one meaning for all prisoners—the gallows. We said good-by to him. He took me aside: 'This is the end, but for me it is the beginning of life.' The next day he was hanged in Flossenburg."[75]

The camp doctor witnessed Bonhoeffer's last minutes and also spoke of his character:

Through the half-open door in one room of the huts I saw Pastor Bonhoeffer, before taking off his prison garb, kneeling on the floor praying fervently to his God. I was most deeply moved by the way this unusually lovable man prayed, so devout and so certain that God heard his prayer. At the place of execution, he again said a short prayer and then climbed the steps to the gallows, brave and composed. His death ensued after a few seconds. In almost fifty years that I worked as a doctor, I have hardly ever seen a man die so entirely submissive to the will of God.[76]

The last sermon Bonhoeffer preached on that last fateful day was based on these two texts: "By his wounds we are healed," from Isaiah 53, and "Praise be to the God and Father of our Lord Jesus Christ! In his great mercy he has given us new birth into a living hope through the resurrection of Jesus Christ from the dead," from 1 Peter 1:3.

But the life Bonhoeffer gave for the gospel began years earlier in daily dying. Bonhoeffer died to the self when he returned to Germany from the U.S. and joined forces with those who were resisting the Nazis. It would have been so much easier to stay in the U.S. and so much easier to keep his mouth shut. Further, he died to a life of academic prestige and a future in the hierarchy of the Lutheran Church in the days Hitler was rising into power because he spoke up and out. So, instead of a nice professorship at a German university, Bonhoeffer began teaching at a clandestine seminary where he lectured on discipleship, and those lectures became the book formerly entitled *The Cost of Discipleship*. The original German title, like Bonhoeffer's own faith, was more austere and direct: *Discipleship*. In that volume Bonhoeffer wrote words that made me shudder as a college student as I contemplated a life of following Jesus. Bonhoeffer's words, not as poetic as the original English translation but once again direct and clear, are as follows: "Whenever Christ calls us, his call leads us to death."[77] Bonhoeffer hardly knew that those words of his were prophetic of the lamb-like sacrifice he'd have to give of his own body, but he was prepared because he had been dying daily for decades.

A rich man approached Jesus and he wanted to gain eternal life. Jesus told him to follow the second half of the Ten Commandments, those that focus on loving others. The man chirped up, perhaps with a bit of a puffy chest, that he had done these since he was little boy. Jesus, knowing the rich's man's heart was anchored to his possessions, then said: "You lack one thing. Sell everything you have and give to the poor, and you will have treasure in heaven. Then come, follow me" (Luke 18:18 – 22). The rich man had to die, in lamblike fashion, to his possessions and die to the self that craved and delighted in those possessions. We face the same fork in the road: either we will choose our own way — the way of riches or the way of biased love — or we will die so we can choose Jesus' way. Which road will you take?

The Kingdom.Life is the Cross.Life, the Messiah is the Lamb of God and he calls us to join him at the Cross in a lamb-like sacrifice of the self.

But Jesus isn't just the Lamb of God and we aren't just lamb-like. If Golgotha morphed into Grace, it was because the Lamb himself morphed, and this is the best news ever!

THE LAMB WHO IS THE LION

Kris and I were at a lion park in South Africa, not far from a place called Pilanesberg National Park, a game reserve. We had driven with some friends through Pilanesberg hoping we might see a lion in the wild. We did see baboons and elephants and giraffes and some other animals that show up in the U.S. only in zoos. But no lions. So our friend, Attie Nel, took us to the lion park nearby to see real lions.

It began with a petting zoo where we touched and held some baby lions, and then we heard truly hair-raising stories about how they teach lions to hunt and what happens to a lion when it realizes it's not just a little fellow that gets petted but is actually a ferocious beast.

It was about then that I heard a lion roar, and it shook me. Something inside me was intensely scared by the sound of that lion roar. The male lion in the area behind us had realized something and it let out a roar that reverberated off walls and trees and made my vertebrae tingle.

Lions spend most of their days sleeping and lounging and swatting flies with their tails and rolling over and looking around and just generally being big cats. But when they want to be noticed, when they want the world to know their lionesses are their lionesses and their babies are their babies, when they want you to know their food is their food, they roar. The whole park hears, the whole continent hears, the world backs off, and only a fool takes no notice.

No lamb would ever challenge a lion. Ever.

The lamb has no chance. Ever.

But one Lamb did. One Lamb became the One.Lion, one Lion became One.Lamb. The Lamb of God is also the Lion of Judah and the Lion of Judah is the Lamb of God. What does that mean for you and me as followers of Jesus?

One generation after the hideous injustice of Golgotha, one generation after Jesus had been unjustly slain as the Lamb of God, one of Jesus' closest followers, the apostle John, is found weeping because he yearns for someone who will establish justice in this world. He yearns for the Lord's Prayer, for the Dream of all Dreams to become a living reality. No one, he realizes, is worthy of opening the scroll containing God's plan, so he weeps and weeps. Then suddenly he is told that the "Lion of the tribe of Judah" — the one who paradoxically in the previous chapter of Revelation was the Lamb — is worthy.

Why is the Lamb-Become-Lion and Lion-Become-Lamb worthy? Because he triumphed (see Revelation 5:5). How did he triumph? He has been raised from the dead, he has conquered death, and now the Lamb-Who-Is-Lion is on the throne of God. The cross is not the final word; the final word is Life, the God.Life that raised Jesus from the dead to sit on the throne as the Lion. Amazingly, that Lion's job, this grand finale of books in the Bible tells us, is to install Jesus' followers as a "kingdom and priests" and our task is to "reign on the earth" in God's kingdom.

Do you hear the roar? The Lamb-Who-Is-Lion roars from the distant horizon. The Lion has been inside the grave and down into the depths of death, but God raised him from the dead and is now roaring. He came back to life and he ascended into the throne room of God, where he reigns. From that distant horizon, the Raised One now roars. He roars to let us know he is Lord. He roars to let us know that Caesar is not Lord, he is. He roars to let us know he's sent the Spirit to make us one and to empower us to live as God's beloved community. He roars to let us know we are gifted to serve in that community. He roars to let us know God loves us. He roars to let us know that justice, love, wisdom, and peace matter to him. He roars to inform us that he's watching. He roars to let us know that he's coming again. He roars to let us know that Death is not the final word.

The last word is the roar of the Lamb-Who-Is-Lion-Who-Is-Life.

That Lion's roar doesn't frighten us. No, that roar gives us confidence to press on with the Cross.Life. That roar empowers us to pick up the cross daily and follow the Lamb-Who-Is-Lion. That roar enables us to fight through our doubts and to struggle through defeats. That roar wakes us up and gets us going and keeps us going straight along the cross path. That roar points the way toward the Kingdom.Life and urges us to give up our One.Life to him. The Cross.Life, the roar tells us time and time again, is about a cross that is empty and about a grave that is empty and about a throne that is full.

If the Lamb becomes a Lion, so too do we. Those who carry the cross can roar too. Our roar echoes the Lion's, who is Lord of the Kingdom. Give your One.Life to the roar.

FINAL WORDS

I wrote this book for people who really do think a Christian is some-one who follows Jesus and for those who want to focus once again on what Jesus meant when he said, "Come follow me." Perhaps you are wondering how you can live out your One.Life for the Kingdom. Life as a Cross.Life. I want to make five brief suggestions:

First, talk to God constantly by worshiping God and by seeking God's will and by interceding for others. Prayer is the way to die to our own wishes and surrender everything to God. We die to what makes sense at times by trusting that God, who is invisible, both wants us to pray and hears us. Jesus prayed often; so can we.

Second, listen to God constantly. Jesus, and all his followers, have learned to listen to and for God's voice in these two ways: by reading the Bible—and by that I mean from cover to cover and not just in snippets of verses—and listening to what God says to us as we read the Bible. Furthermore, in prayer sometimes God speaks to us—what my pastor calls "promptings"—and sometimes we just know that God has spoken and we are to do something about it. Learning to listen to God means learning to die to our voices and the voices of others. Listen for the roar of the Lamb-Who-Is-Lion.

Third, commit to kingdom work locally by asking God's Spirit to empower you and by entering into fellowship with others who follow Jesus in that same Spirit. That local fellowship of followers of Jesus is a church—and whether it's a megachurch or a house church, a denomination or an organic church doesn't matter. A fundamental point that is found everywhere in the New Testament is that Jesus' kingdom is to be embodied in a church of ordinary people—just like you and me—who celebrate the Lord's Supper, who follow the Lord's way together, and who embody the kingdom life as much as they can. This is the primary location for our kingdom work. Devoting ourselves to a local fellowship means we have died to our plans and our own way of doing things.

Fourth, to keep Jesus' kingdom vision in front of you at every moment, I suggest you recite daily the Jesus Creed of loving God and loving others (below) and the Lord's Prayer (next page):

Hear, O Israel:
The Lord our God, the Lord is one.
Love the Lord your God with all your heart
and with all your soul
and with all your mind
and with all your strength.

The second is this:

Love your neighbor as yourself.
There is no commandment greater than these.

Fifth, don't be afraid to tell others about the kingdom vision of Jesus. Telling others about Jesus means we have to die to telling others about ourselves all the time. All the early followers of Jesus called this telling the story of Jesus "evangelism," but what they meant by that was not haranguing people or scaring people or condemning people but very simply telling them about Jesus and his kingdom vision. It means telling them about the life of Jesus, the teachings of Jesus, the cross of Jesus, the resurrection of Jesus, and Jesus' sending of the Spirit at Pentecost to make us the people God wants us to be.

Interlude

There is only one way to conclude this book on the kingdom dream of Jesus. And it is something Jesus gave to you and to me to recite daily to remind ourselves of his kingdom dream: The Lord's Prayer.

Our Father which art in heaven,
Hallowed be thy name.
Thy kingdom come.
Thy will be done in earth, as it is in heaven.
Give us this day our daily bread.
And forgive us our debts, as we forgive our debtors.
And lead us not into temptation, but deliver us from evil:
For thine is the kingdom, and the power, and the glory, for ever.
Amen.

AFTER WORDS

This book emerged out of conversations and reading and prayer over the last three decades, but its more immediate context is my teaching the Jesus of Nazareth class at North Park University. Interaction with these fine students influences every page of this book.

Speaking and preaching in churches across the U.S., in Canada, Denmark, and South Africa has taught me much, and I want to thank the pastors and churches for their hospitality and grace. I must mention Wes Olmstead, Mie Skak Johansen, Attie Nel, Marius Nel, Tom Smith, Coenie Burger, Willem Pretorius, Theo and Wilma Geyser, and Andre Serfontein.

One church deserves special thanks: Irving Bible Church, and I am grateful to Andy McQuitty, Steve and Jackie Roese, and others too numerous to list here for the hospitality and encouragement they have given me over the years. One weekend I was privileged to present the initial findings of *One.Life* and it was a weekend I shall never forget.

Kris, my wife, is my companion and constant reader and ever-faithful critic, and this book owes much to her wisdom and responses and gut-level ideas. In addition, I wish to thank a number who read the book in part: Chris Ridgeway, who was not only my graduate assistant for two years but one whom I could bounce ideas off of that either found their way into this book or got clipped; J. R. Woodward, who wrote up a few pages of comments and questions; and Margaret Feinberg, who went beyond my requests to push me to cleaner prose. More suggestions came from J. R. Briggs, Tom Smith,

Marie Liefblad, Terry Erickson, Joe Modica, Wade Hodges, Andy Rowell, Don Golden, Josh Graves, and Lee Camp. My colleagues at North Park, including Ginny Olsen, Jim Dekker, Boaz Johnson, Brad Nassif, Joel Willitts, Mary Veeneman, and Greg Clark in one way or another, often when they didn't even know it, have helped me to sharpen ideas in this book. I am always grateful to the Evangelical Covenant Church, to North Park University, and to the conditions they have made available to me that permit me to write and speak. My special thanks to David and Linda Parkyn, and as well to Joe Jones and Charles Peterson, a team of wonderful administrators who make our work easier because they do their jobs so well.

Greg Daniel, my agent, made an important suggestion that shifted an emphasis of the book; John Raymond, my editor at Zondervan, is a longtime friend and insightful observer of all things Christian, and he sent drafts back to me and told me to get it better. Becky Philpott at Zondervan reminds me why I am so grateful to editors.

My prayer for this book is simple: I pray that God will use this book to create more followers of Jesus.

NOTES

1. www.cdbaby.com/cd/TomRorem
2. A friend of mine, J. R. Woodward, blogs at a site he calls *Dream Awakener* (http://jrwoodward.net), and I first became aware of this expression there.
3. Wikipedia, "Ubuntu (philosophy)." The citations from Desmond Tutu and Nelson Mandela are from that Wikipedia entry. Tutu discusses *ubuntu* in several of his books, including *God Has a Dream: A Vision of Hope for Our Time* (with Douglas Abrams; New York: Doubleday Image, 2005), 24–29.
4. http://en.wikipedia.org/wiki/Ubuntu_(philosophy)
5. Ibid.
6. Ed Dobson, *The Year of Living Like Jesus* (Grand Rapids: Zondervan, 2009).
7. Title of Bill Maher's comedy/documentary film. The word combines the words *religion* and *ridiculous*.
8. Lee Camp, *Mere Discipleship: Radical Christianity in a Rebellious World* (2nd ed.; Grand Rapids: Brazos, 2008), 39.
9. www.youtube.com/watch?v=gUdrYDk8rVA; /watch?v=grBByc7t3Fs; / watch?v=lvOlA4egNvk; /watch?v=sTngTuGHbrM
10. See these pictures by Jules Morgan: http://www.julesmorgan.com/index.php/news-topmenu–8/5-personal/29-khayaletsha-site-c.html, accessed May 28, 2009.
11. Tom Davis, *Fields of the Fatherless* (Colorado Springs: David C. Cook, 2008) 34, 56.
12. Actually, we begin with Mary's Magnificat (Luke 1:46–55), move next to Zechariah's Benedictus (1:67–79), and then move over to his son's, John the Baptist's, own words of what real repentance looks like (3:10–14), and we would also need to balance this justice vision with the cross and resurrection at its center (and we look at Luke 9:18–27 and 24:45–49). Then we move into Acts 2, with both the power of Pentecost and the justice community it created in 2:42–47. The just community is never abandoned for a purely spiritual salvation.
13. Randy Harris, *God Work: Confessions of a Standup Theologian* (Abilene, Texas: Leafwood, 2009), 100.
14. If you don't know it, here's a link: http://www.cyberhymnal.org/htm/i/t/i

/itiswell.htm. Here are the words: http://www.hymns.me.uk/when-peace-like-a-river-favorite-hymn.htm.

15. Luke 2:14; Matt. 5:9; Luke 19:38, 42. The lines in the next paragraph are from John 14:27.

16. Romans 15:33; 16:20.

17. http://www.walking4water.org/.

18. http://www.vimeo.com/loveisfree/videos.

19. Andy Stanley, *The Best Question Ever: A Revolutionary Approach to Decision-Making* (Sisters, Oregon: Multnomah, 2004).

20. *The Best Question Ever: A Revolutionary Approach to Decision Making* (Sisters, Ore.: Multnomah, 2004).

21. From the Babylonian Talmud, Shabbat 31a.

22. C. S. Lewis, *Mere Christianity* (New York: Macmillan, 1956), 89.

23. I heard this in a sermon at Willow Creek Community Church, South Barrington, Illinois, January 16, 2010.

24. Francis Chan, *The Forgotten God: Reversing our Tragic Neglect of the Holy Spirit* (Colorado Springs: David C. Cook, 2009).

25. Jean M. Twenge, *Generation Me* (New York: Free Press, 2007).

26. Craig Keener, *The Historical Jesus of the Gospels* (Grand Rapids: Eerdmans, 2009), 384–385.

27. George Washington, *Rules of Civility* (Charlottesville: University of Virginia Press, 2003), 62 (#54).

28. Jim Wallis, *Rediscovering Values: A Moral Compass for the New Economy* (New York: Howard Books, 2010), 44. The story about the Bible full of holes can be found at: www.30goodminutes.org/csec/New_letter/Apr04web.pdf, accessed January 29, 2010.

29. Andrea Jaeger, *First Service: Following God's Calling and Finding Life's Purpose* (Deerfield Beach, Florida: Health Communications, 2004).

30. The story has been told well by Catherine Claire Larson, *As We Forgive: Stories of Reconciliation from Rwanda* (Grand Rapids: Zondervan, 2009).

31. From *The Illustrated London News*, 7/16/1910.

32. Huston Smith, *Tales of Wonder: Adventures Chasing the Divine: An Autobiography* (with Jerry Paine; San Francisco: HarperOne, 2009), 109, 113.

33. Richard Stearns, *A Hole in Our Gospel* (Nashville: Thomas Nelson, 2009), 31, 38, 43.

34. In this chapter I have relied upon Donna Freitas, *Sex and the Soul* (New York: Oxford, 2008), quoting here from p. 173; Laura Sessions Stepp, *Unhooked: How Young Women Pursue Sex, Delay Love and Lose at Both* (New York: Riverhead Books, 2008); and Joe S. McIlhaney, Freda McKissic Bush, *Hooked: New Science on How Casual Sex Is Affecting Our Children* (Chicago: Northfield Publishing, 2008).

35. Stepp, *Unhooked*, 9.

36. Ibid., 33.

37. Erwin Raphael McManus, *Soul Cravings* (Nashville: Thomas Nelson, 2006), 7.

38. Stepp, *Unhooked*, 240.

39. Ibid., 258.
40. Ibid., 258–259.
41. Ibid., 261.
42. Freitas, *Sex and the Soul*, xv.
43. Ibid., 153.
44. Ibid.
45. Stepp, *Unhooked*, xiv.
46. For further study, see D. P. Hollinger, *The Meaning of Sex: Christian Ethics and the Moral Life* (Grand Rapids: Baker Academic, 2009).
47. http://www.cnn.com/2009/LIVING/personal/08/18/tf.women.need.a.man/index.html, accessed August 19, 2009.
48. Stepp, *Unhooked*, 69.
49. Ibid., 40.
50. Freitas, *Sex and the Soul*, 130.
51. Stepp, *Unhooked*, 187.
52. Ibid., 205.
53. Freitas, *Sex and the Soul*, 5–9.
54. From http://www.dailymail.co.uk/femail/article–1195344/My-year-sex-Hephzibah-Anderson-took-dramatic -- liberating -- decision-So-did-help-real-love.html, accessed August 24, 2009.
55. Denis de Rougemont, *Love in the Western World* (trans. Montgomery Belgion; rev. ed.; Princeton: Princeton University Press, 1983), 305.
56. Ibid.
57. For S. Kierkegaard, see the anthology of A. A. and L. R. Kass, *Wing to Wing, Oar to Oar: Readings on Courting and Marrying* (Notre Dame, Indiana: University of Notre Dame Press, 2000), 123.
58. James Brown, *The Role of a Lifetime: Reflections on Faith, Family, and Significant Living* (with Nathan Whitaker; foreword by Tony Dungy; New York: Faith Words, 2009), 110.
59. Kathleen Norris, *The Quotidian Mysteries: Laundry, Liturgy and "Women's Work"* (1998 Madaleva Lecture in Spirituality; New York: Paulist, 1998), 12.
60. Rob Bell, *Sex God: Exploring the Endless Connections between Sexuality and Spirituality* (Grand Rapids: Zondervan, 2008); John Piper, *This Momentary Marriage: A Parable of Permanence* (Wheaton: Crossway, 2009).
61. I rely here on the excellent biography from Joan D. Hedrick, *Harriet Beecher Stowe: A Life* (New York: Oxford University Press, 1994), 207–209, 234, 303. One cannot fail to mention that Stowe acquired sympathy for the slave through her own servants.
62. F. Buechner, *Beyond Words: Daily Readings in the ABC's of Faith* (SanFrancisco: HarperSanFrancisco, 2004), 405.
63. Parker Palmer, *Let Your Life Speak: Listening for the Voice of Vocation* (San Francisco: Jossey-Bass, 1999).
64. Andy Crouch, *Culture Making: Recovering our Creative Calling* (Downers Grove: IVP, 2008).

65. A good book on this topic is N. T. Wright, *Surprised by Hope* (San Francisco: HarperOne, 2008).

66. Rodney Stark, *What Americans Really Believe* (Waco, Tex.: Baylor University Press, 2008), 69–74.

67. Harper Lee, *To Kill a Mockingbird* (New York: HarperCollins, 1993), 50.

68. Dale Allison Jr., *Resurrecting Jesus: The Earliest Christian Tradition after its Interpreters* (New York: T & T Clark, 2005), 99.

69. See Alan E. Bernstein, *The Formation of Hell: Death and Retribution in the Ancient and Early Christian Worlds* (Ithaca: Cornell University Press, 1993), and on Gehenna see pp. 167–172.

70. Perhaps the most well-known sketch of annihilationism is that of evangelical John R. W. Stott, *Evangelical Essentials: A Liberal-Evangelical Dialogue* (with David Edwards; Downers Grove: IVP, 1988), 312–329.

71. See *The Great Divorce* (San Francisco: HarperSanFrancisco, 1973). A recent book, under the pseudonym of Gregory Macdonald, which stands for Gregory of Nyssa and George Macdonald, both of whom were Christian universalists, argues that there is such a thing as evangelical universalism. See *The Evangelical Universalist* (the author's name is Robin Parry; London: SPCK, 2008).

72. I rely here on pages 106–130 of A. Newberg and M. R. Waldman, *How God Changes Your Brain: Breakthrough Findings from a Leading Neuroscientist* (New York: Ballantine, 2009), 107.

73. Tim Keller, *The Prodigal God: Recovering the Heart of the Christian Faith* (New York: Dutton, 2008), 18.

74. For a fine new book on this topic, see Judith Couchman, *The Mystery of the Cross: Bringing Ancient Christian Images to Life* (Downers Grove: IVP, 2009).

75. From the Introduction to Bonhoeffer's *Life Together* (trans. J. Doberstein; New York: Harper & Row, 1954), 13. For a fuller account, see E. Bethge, *Dietrich Bonhoeffer: A Life* (rev. ed.; Minneapolis: Fortress, 2000), 921–933.

76. E. Bethge, *Dietrich Bonhoeffer: A Life*, 927–928.

77. This from *Discipleship* in the official edition of Bonhoeffer's works. See *Discipleship* (DBW 4; various translators Barbara Green and Reinhard Krauss; Minneapolis: Fortress, 2001). The earlier English had "When Christ calls a man, he bids him come and die." The German reads: *Jeder Ruf Christi fährt in den Tod*. It might be translated as follows: "Every summons of Christ leads to death."

The Blue Parakeet

Rethinking How You Read the Bible

Scot McKnight, author of The Jesus Creed

Why Can't I Just Be a Christian?

Parakeets make delightful pets. We cage them or clip their wings to keep them where we want them. Scot McKnight contends that many, conservatives and liberals alike, attempt the same thing with the Bible. We all try to tame it.

McKnight's *The Blue Parakeet* has emerged at the perfect time to cool the flames of a world on fire with contention and controversy. It calls Christians to a way to read the Bible that leads beyond old debates and denominational battles. It calls Christians to stop taming the Bible and to let it speak anew for a new generation.

In his books *The Jesus Creed* and *Embracing Grace*, Scot McKnight established himself as one of America's finest Christian thinkers, an author to be reckoned with.

In *The Blue Parakeet*, McKnight again touches the hearts and minds of today's Christians, this time challenging them to rethink how to read the Bible, not just to puzzle it together into some systematic theology but to see it as a Story that we're summoned to enter and to carry forward in our day.

In his own inimitable style, McKnight sets traditional and liberal Christianity on its ear, leaving readers equipped, encouraged, and emboldened to be the people of faith they long to be.

Available in stores and online!

Connect with Scot on Facebook, Twitter, or his blog:

http://www.facebook.com/home.php?#!/scot.mcknight
http://twitter.com/scotmcknight
http://patheos.com/community/jesuscreed/